People of the Cedars

THE INHERITANCE

Ken Hanna

Leopard Press
Johannesburg, South Africa

Leopard Press
18 Arniston, TheWillows Estate
Kelland, Randburg 2194
South Africa
publisher@leopardpress.co.za

Ordering Information:
Quantity sales. Special discounts are available on quantity purchases by
corporations, associations, and others. For details, contact the
publisher at the address above.

Biblical quotations are mainly from the New Revised Standard Version
Bible: Catholic Edition, copyright © 1989, 1993 the Division of
Christian Education of the National Council of the Churches of Christ
in the United States of America. Used by permission. All rights
reserved.

People of the Cedars: The Inheritance/ Ken Hanna. —1st ed.
ISBN 978-1-9200821-2-3

Contents

With gratitude to Father Michael Chebli for the outline of this book.

Father Michael Chebli – Maronite Lebanese Missionary – (left) with the author at the Retirement Village Home of Religious in Broummena Lebanon, May 2015. Father Chebli has studied the Bible in Arabic, English, Aramaic, Hebrew, Spanish, Portuguese, Greek and Italian.

And to my eldest daughter Rene Stevenson for editing and layout.

Foreword: Kabalan Frangieh: Ambassador of Lebanon to SA

There is no doubt that "The Inheritance" is a book that encapsulates the history and present of the country of the Cedars.

Ken Hanna who embodies the connection between Lebanon and South Africa shows once again that he is the keeper of the collective memory of the Lebanese-South African Community.

His heart is stamped on every word and idea in this book.

He managed to gather the most important achievements and recognized the most significant individuals who contributed to the enhancement of the Lebanese Community in South Africa and the diaspora.

Ken Hanna is a living example of the choice emigrants had to make, if we cannot live in Lebanon, let Lebanon live in us.

As the Ambassador of Lebanon to South Africa, I express my deep gratitude for the work done to write this book which is considered a reference to a better understanding of the presence of the Lebanese community in South Africa and the diaspora.

It is clear that Ken Hanna's contribution to the relation between Lebanon, Lebanese in South Africa and the diaspora is invaluable.

His dedication and passion set an example to the new generations.

This book is a statement that we all have a mission and a challenge to bring our members of the community closer to each other and closer to their country of origin.

It is a mission to raise the message that Lebanon embodies; a message of living together and standing by each other.

Message from Fr Maurice Chidiac

"Well done good and faithful servant" (Matthew 25:21)

Dearest Ken,

I found in the parable of the talents (Mt 25:14-30) all that I would like to tell you.

In this parable, our Lord Jesus speaks about a master "calling" his servants and "entrusting" them with "talents", each one "according to his abilities".

No doubt, you have a "calling": long ago from God, anchored by your devout Maronite Lebanese family and flourished in the heart of your community.

You have been "entrusted" with "talents" and you responded well. Always proud of your Phoenician, Maronite, Lebanese and Becharre roots.

Always with admirable perseverance, unwavering patience to gather information, to write it down and to promote it.

Always loyal to your church and the priests who have a lot of respect for you and for your generous and unselfish dedication.

"According to your ability", through long and passionate hard work, your unique journey has led you, for more than 60 years, from the newsletter "The Cedar Leaf" to your first book "People of the Cedars" and now to "The Inheritance".

"After a long time" the master came back: "Well done good and faithful servant. Since you were faithful in small matters, I will give you great responsibilities... Enter into the joy of your master".

Echoing these beautiful and powerful words of our Saviour, and from the bottom of my heart, I thank you for responding to the Divine generosity bestowed on you in the way you have, and I pray that you rejoice from His divine promises.

God's richest Blessings,
With all my love and respect,

Fr Maurice Chidiac MLM
Superior of the Maronite Lebanese Mission in South Africa

*"The righteous flourish like the palm tree,
and grow like a cedar in Lebanon."*

PSALM 92:12

Introduction

As a descendant of immigrants I have two wings: my ancestral home in Lebanon and my country of birth, South Africa. It is on these wings that I have learned to fly.

The wings of my grandparents – like many who fled Lebanon escaping persecution and poverty at the end of the nineteenth century – were at first fledging: unsteady and vulnerable, carrying as they did the sorrows of leaving the Motherland and loved ones.

Their landing in the strange continent of Africa brought many challenges and hardships: uncertainty, unfamiliar language and culture, famine, drought, financial failures, poverty, discrimination and the pain of dislocation and alienation inherent in the immigrant experience.

Building nests for their offspring was a true labour of love. But despite all odds, we survived and our wings and those of our children and grandchildren grew strong.

And over the decades we thrived. Drawing on our inner strength, and the strength of our faith, values and community we learned to soar with pride, accomplishment and dignity.

I believe this is our *Inheritance* – the special and unique vocation and contribution of the Lebanese in the world today – our ethos, spirit, heritage and identity.

This book is the story of those wings. I have written it through the lens of my Lebanese South African heritage, Maronite Christian faith and personal story.

Touching on the pre, ancient, biblical and modern history of the Lebanese, I look at how these have shaped the Lebanese ethos, culture, spirituality and psyche today. *Lebanity* – our Lebanese heritage and identity – rests on four pillars: Family, Faith, Finance and Fellowship.

And so I share with you the story of my Maronite faith, beginning with our patron Saint Maron, and the first Christians in the Holy Mountains of Lebanon, followed by a brief history of Maronity through the ages, including the unique historical and current relationship between Maronite Christians and Rome.

To illustrate the Lebanese values of Finance and Fellowship, I share stories, biographies and achievements of a few Lebanese business, philanthropic, literary and community luminaries.

I look at the pain and legacy of the immigrant experience and the achievements of the Lebanese in the diaspora today, and in South Africa in particular.

I have included a historical timeline of the Lebanese from the first inhabitants in what is modern day Lebanon, to the most recent events in the country – to provide a backdrop and context for understanding and clarity.

I conclude with my understanding of our *Inheritance*: a people who have thrived and flourished wherever we have landed; a nation – at home and in the diaspora – with the deep values of *Lebanity*: friendship, hospitality, strength in adversity, community and more; a people who through suffering and persecution strive wholeheartedly (albeit at times failing dismally) to create peaceful co-existence, inter-faith dialogue, tolerance and respect for diversity and difference.

This is not a history book, but rather a personal journal, a collection of reflections and stories, poetry, opinion pieces, photographs, anecdotes and quotes.

My hope is that the spirit of the Lebanese – and especially our unique vocation and inheritance in The Holy Land and around the world – shines through these stories and pages.

So, please join me as I explore the dynamic world of the Lebanese and rediscover our unique and Sacred Vocation.

Insha'Allah.

"I love you, my brother, whoever you are - whether you worship in a church, kneel in your temple, or pray in your mosque. You and I are children of one faith, for the diverse paths of religion are fingers of the loving hand of the one Supreme Being, a hand extended to all, offering completeness of spirit to all, eager to receive all."

Gibran Kahlil Gibran: Treasured Writing, Castle Books

"People of the Cedars": Genesis of the Name

When we mention "People of the Cedars" we think of the Lebanese people. How did the name arise?

Sometime during 1970 I was given a mandate to start the "Cedar Leaf" – a news publication serving the Lebanese South African community.

Some 25 years later the idea of publishing a book arose.
It needed a name. The one chosen was "People of the Cedars".

During the 1970's the World Lebanese Cultural Union (WLCU) was in the ascendency. It was formally known as the World Lebanese Union, but had to change the name because of pressure from Brazil who thought it might be political. This Union was under the umbrella of the Ministry of Foreign Affairs in Lebanon.

There were those in the Diaspora who were not happy as they thought the orientation was more sympathetic to the East, Syria, Russia, Iran and China. The Diaspora, in the main, were more with the West: the United States, Britain, France and Israel.

The Lebanese in South Africa were right in the middle. We did not want to upset the applecart so we created a movement, albeit very small, known as the "People of the Cedars". It would be all embracing – like the footprint of the Elephant, which is large enough to include the footprints of all the other animals.

In our families and in our community there are those who are Buddhist, Atheist, Maronite Catholic, Melkite Catholic, Roman Catholic, Evangelical Christian, Pentecostal, Agnostic, Muslim, Jewish, New Age and Greek Orthodox. So we had to look to a common denominator:

This is our "Lebanity": our Lebanese identity, spirituality and heritage. "People of the Cedars" symbolizes and is synonymous with this encompassing vision and ethos. It is a name to which friends of the "People of the Cedars" can relate. Over the years we have tried to expound our vision and our mission.

So why not *just* a Maronite Publication?

Whilst I am a practicing Maronite, I realized that the Community dynamics had changed since we began. The needs and the aspirations were very different. The key:

Maronity, today, is for all, not just Lebanese.

So "People of the Cedars" and "Cedar Leaf" have changed with the times.

No more large editions. No more big functions.

Everything smaller. From macro to micro. Now small groups. Families getting together.

There is another interesting phenomenon. The world has become a small place. With technology, the Internet, Facebook and other social media, the Lebanese scattered throughout the World are able to connect.

The all-embracing idea and ideal that Lebanon has created can now be widely spread and shared across the globe. Always looking to Lebanon.

So we believe we have seen the gap:

The "Cedar Leaf" newsletter: Small. The Inheritance: Going Global.

CHAPTER 1

Lebanese Prehistory

Lebanon's prehistoric heritage dates back over one million years. More than 400 sites in Lebanon have revealed the presence of prehistoric humans. These include artefacts from the first hunter-gatherers, shedding light on their lifestyle and evolution, to the invention of agriculture and domestication of animals, which led to the settlement of the human species. These archaeological sites contain fascinating flint tools, human and animal bones, pottery and jewellery which tell the story of the first humans that occupied the territories constituting Lebanon today. Ksar Akil near Beirut is one of the most important Paleolithic sites in Eurasia. Human fossils and shell beads found in this rock shelter date the presence of early humans (as opposed to Neanderthals) to around 42 000 years ago.

The Stone Age in Lebanon – 180 000 BC as depicted by Fadlallah Dagher[1]

[1], An "Illustrated history of the Lebanon", Nayla de Freige and Maria Saad, illustrated by Fadlallah Dagher, 1987[1]

Five UNESCO World Heritage Sites

Lebanon's rich ancient history is preserved at over 400 archaeological sites, five of which are UNESCO Cultural World Heritage sites.

Anjar:

Anjar – a town in the Bekaa valley of Lebanon's Zahle district – is the site of the ruins of a palace built during the Umayyad Civilization by Caliph Walid I at the beginning of the 8th century. Excavations revealed a fortified city filled with 42 towers and walls.

Umayyad Palace at Anjar

Baalbek

This ancient Phoenician city served as a site of worship for a triad of deities: Jupiter, Venus and Bacchus. The Temple of Bacchus is one of the largest Roman temple ruins in the world. It is so well-preserved that carvings of lions and bulls are still visible.

The temple of Bacchus, Baalbek

Byblos

Byblos is the oldest continuously inhabited city in the world. It was first inhabited between 8,800 and 7,000 BC.

Tyre

Tyre was one of the two leading city-states in Phoenicia, and the most important seaport. It is believed the famous Phoenician purple dye was invented here and it is also known as the birthplace of Dido and Europa. It is among the largest cities and ports in modern day Lebanon. The majority of ruins date to the Roman period. Notable structures include the 12th century cathedral built by the Venetians, Roman baths, Roman arena, and the walls of the ancient Crusader castle.

Roman ruins at Tyre, South Lebanon

Qadisha Valley and the Forest of the Cedars of God

Qadisha Valley (which means "Holy" Valley, also called the Valley of Saints), is one of the world's most significant early Christian monastic settlements where communities have existed for centuries protected by magnificent rugged landscapes with dramatic views. The valley is located at the foot of the North of Mount-Lebanon chain. The rocky cliffs among the valleys are considered a place for meditation and worship. This area is also considered to have the largest collection of Christian monasteries and hermitages since Christianity first spread.

Near these monastic settlements are the Cedars of Lebanon which – myth has it – were planted by the hand of God, hence the name "Arz el-Rab" "Forest of the Cedars of God". In Biblical times, cedar trees were both precious and prestigious, affordable only by the rich. King

Solomon's temple was built by King Hiram of Phoenicia with wood from the Holy Cedars and the Egyptian Pharaoh Tutankhamen had furniture in his tomb made of Phoenician cedar.

The Holy Qadisha Valley

From the Cradle of Civilization (Lebanon) to the Cradle of Humankind (South Africa)

Reconstruction of the early Hominid "Homo Naledi"

During 2015 I had the rare privilege of visiting not only Lebanon, but also 'The Cradle of Humankind' in Maropeng near Muldersdrift in South Africa, to view the great world heritage site and premier display of newly discovered fossil: Homo Naledi.

When my grandparents – Kahlil Hanna Schehadie Kairouz and his wife Khola of the Tawk family – left Lebanon at the end of the nineteenth century, little did they realize that they would become farmers in

Muldersdrift South Africa, nor that they would be farming in one of the "hotspots" of the Cradle of Humankind.

Never in their wildest dreams did they think that one of their 18 grandchildren (myself), their great grandchild (my daughter Carol) and their great-great grandchild (my granddaughter Claire) would visit the area over 120 years later to explore the world of "Paleoanthropology" – the dawn of humanity.

With my Granddaughter Claire at 'The Cradle of Humankind', Maropeng

My grandparents were carrying a history that goes back 180 000 years to Neanderthal Man.

Around 40,000 years ago Neanderthal man disappeared and his place was taken by Homo sapiens – the modern human species.
It is fascinating to experience how simply Nayla de Freige and Maria Saad unfold this history:

The Stone Age, the beginning of agriculture, the discovery of copper, the birth of the city states, the Phoenicians: Kings of Mediterranean trade; Phoenician craftsmen; all the conquerors of Lebanon including Alexander the Great, the Romans and the Ottomans.

It was during the time of the Ottoman Empire that my grandparents emigrated from Lebanon. They left behind their history, culture and religious home – Maronite Christianity in its pristine form – never to return.

The Cradle of Humankind

During our visit to "The Cradle of Humankind" we embarked on a journey back in time to when the world began. A timeline highlighting some of the major events in our earth's history.

The adventure began in the present and continued on a trip back through time, retracing the various stages of the creation of our earth, through snow, ice, water and the formation of the earth's crust. When the earth was a fiery ball of molten rock.

The birth of the cradle, the path to humanity; what it means to be human.
The characteristics that make us human with links to the modern world: free will, the capacity to self-reflect, our imagination, tool making, cooking, music, writing.
The gradual build-up of human/ environmental interaction over time.

The great debate on the theory of Darwinism: that man evolved from the ape species and was not created by Almighty God in his own image and likeness with a soul, intellect and free will.

Paleoanthropologists

As we try to discover our human heritage and inheritance we have to explore the minds of not only paleoanthropologists (the artists of the discipline) but also astronomers, religious leaders and botanists.

We also need to have a look at Darwinism, the "Big Bang" theory and the creation of our universe. What better vantage point than Lebanon and South Africa?

The possibility of linking humans with early apes by descent became clear only after 1859 with the publication of Charles Darwin's "Origin of Species".
Doctor Raymond Dart, Professor Robert Broom, Professor Errol Tobias and latterly, Professor Lee Burger of the University of the Witwatersrand, Johannesburg, have tried to uncover, explain and explore our human existence and broaden our understanding.

With the fossilized skull of the 'Taung child' discovered in 1924, Dr Dart tried to explain the transition between apes and man.

Robert Broom – with the findings at Sterkfontein, near Krugersdorp, South Africa, and the skull of 'Mrs Ples' – argued that we originate from Hominoids and not apes.

Dr Lee Burger was delighted and overwhelmed at the discovery of 'Homo Naledi' in Maropeng – a species with very human characteristics.

It is generally agreed that the forerunner of anatomically modern humans evolved in Africa – and more specifically South Africa – 50,000 years ago.

How, then, can human evolution be understood from a Christian perspective?

Darwinism and Christianity

Catholic Archbishop of Durban, South Africa, Denis Hurley (Oblate of Mary Immaculate) writing in 2003 about God's "Special gift to Humans" says:

> *"About 15 billion years ago a cosmic blast occurred that we have come to believe and call the "BIG BANG". Our universe was on its way. God was in it. Guiding it and governing it.*
> *It was the first creative expression of His divine presence that we know. We give thanks to God for His presence amongst us (Jesus in the Eucharist) through the spectacular mystery of creation and the sanctifying mystery of salvation which we celebrate with great joy."*[2]

---

[2] Author's personal meeting with Archbishop Denis Hurley, Durban, 1970s

Also out of South Africa, the Christian Astronomer Professor David Block, who grew up in Krugersdorp, writes:

"*Behold a universe so immense that I am lost in it. I no longer know where I am. I am just nothing at all. Our world is terrifying in its insignificance. And yet, the universe, has to be as large as it is just to support life on earth*". [3]

Nobel Physics Laureate, 1978, Arno A. Penzias writes:

"*Astronomy leads us to a unique universe that was created out of nothing and delicately balanced to provide exactly the conditions required to support life. In the absence of an absurdly improbable accident, the observation of modern science seems to suggest an underlying, one might say "Supernatural" Plan.*

> **Lebanese proverb:**
>
> When you return from a trip, bring back something for your family -- even if it is only a stone.

---

3 Dr David Block's notes on two lectures attended by the writer.

CHAPTER 2

Timeline of Phoenician – Lebanese History

Lebanon has a complex, intriguing (and often painful) history of conquests, occupation and colonization that extends over thousands of years. A brief outline will help us understand not only how each successive civilization has contributed a bright colour to the cultures, traditions and religions that make up the rich tapestry of Lebanon today, but also how mammoth a triumph it has been for the Lebanese to overcome adversity and create a unique Nation and Heritage.

Date	Key Events
Phoenician Era	
BC 4000	City of Sidon founded.
Circa 3000	The area including **present day Lebanon** (as well as Syria and Northern Israel) first appears in recorded history, as Phoenicia – one of the greatest ancient civilizations of history.
2750	Tyre the primary city of Phoenicia is founded.
1800-1400	**Egyptian Empire** Approx. BC 1800 Egyptians take control of Phoenicia.
16th - 17th century	**Babylonian Rule in Mesopotamia** Hammurabi (1792-1750) was King of the 1st Babylonian Dynasty
1100	Phoenician alphabet invented.

Approx 980-947	King Hiram – Phoenician King of Tyre and David King of Israel rule. The two monarchs, who believe in different gods, manage to set aside their differences and create a mutually beneficial diplomatic relationship. This strong relationship continues with King David's son (Solomon) after he dies.
857	First temple in Jerusalem built by King Solomon, with Hiram's workers.
930	End of the third Kingdom of Solomon.
875-608	**Assyrian Rule** Assyrian's break Phoenician monopoly on trade and rule from 875-608.
800-600	Second stage of Phoenician colonization where trading-posts become full colonies throughout the Mediterranean.
825 or 814	Elissa, Princess of Tyre (Phoenicia), flees to Africa and establishes Carthage.
751	Isaiah is born.
586	First destruction of The Temple in Jerusalem.
587-74	Tyre rebels and for thirteen years 587-574 resists siege by the troops of Nebuchadnezzar. After this long siege, the city capitulates; its king is dethroned, and its citizens enslaved.
	Persian Empire
539	The Achaemenids end Babylonian rule when Cyrus, founder of the Persian Empire, captures Babylon in 539-38. Phoenicia passes into Persian hands.
529-522	Cambyses, Cyrus's son and successor, continues his father's policy of conquest and in BC 529 becomes suzerain of Syria, Lebanon and Egypt.
333	Persian Empire falls to Alexander the Great, King of Macedonia. He attacks Asia Minor, defeats the Persian

	troops, and advances toward the Lebanese coast. Initially the Phoenician cities make no attempt to resist, and recognize his suzerainty. However, when Alexander tries to offer a sacrifice to Melkart, Tyre's god, the city resists. A siege of Tyre begins.
Approx 322	**Alexander the Great takes Tyre.** After 7 months of siege, Tyre gives in. 2,000 men are crucified, 30,000 are sold as prisoners. Phoenicia plays a far less prominent role in trade following this conquest. The culture is heavily influenced by Hellenistic culture.
301-195	Tyre, as all other Phoenician cities, belongs to the Ptolemies, rulers of Hellenistic Egypt.
64	In 64 BC, Pompey the Great conquers Phoenicia and it becomes part of the Roman province of Syria. Beirut becomes an important centre under Herod the Great and splendid temples are built at Baalbek.
5 BC	**Birth of Jesus Christ**
AD 28	The visit and teachings of Jesus of Nazareth at Sidon and Tyre.
50	Saint Paul begins his third Apostolic mission and preaches in Tyre.
	4th Century AD – Roman Empire crumbles. **Christianity spreads throughout Lebanon**
Approx 350	St Maron born in Cyrrhus, a small town near Antioch.
Approx 410	St Maron dies.
410-420 AD	The Phoenicians of Jebbet Becharre and Jebbet Mnaytrah convert to Christianity through Abraham the hermit, disciple of St Maron.

451	Council of Chalcedon proclaims the Christological doctrine that Christ is both human and divine.
452	Beit Maron Monastery (House of Maron) built on the Orontes River on request of Pope Leo.
517-540	350 Maronite Christians killed by Monophysites (Christians who believe God was only divine) during bloody conflict. Countless others become refugees. Many Maronites take refuge in the mountains of Lebanon.

For almost 3 centuries Maronity flourishes in Lebanon – particularly in the Cedars where it is protected by the mountainous terrain

| 551 | Beirut destroyed by an earthquake and tsunami. 30,000 killed in the city alone and, along the Phoenician coast, total casualties close to 250,000. |

7th Century: Umayyad Dynasty

First hereditary dynasty of Islam following Muhammad – credited with the Arab conquest that created an Islamic empire stretching from the Indus Valley to Southern France. Ruins are found in Anjar. It ushers in a rich period of Islamic art, architecture, learning and culture that continues to flourish in Lebanon today.

632-34	Calling for a jihad (holy war) against non-Muslims, Muhammad's successor Caliph Abu Bakr brings Islam to area surrounding Lebanon.
Approx 630	A group of autonomous Maronite communities settle in Mount Lebanon and the surrounding highlands following the conquest of Syria by the Arab Caliphate. They are dubbed maradah (rebels).
685	St. John Maron appointed first Patriarch of the Maronite Church.
694	Byzantine Emperor destroys Beit Maron killing 500 Maronite monks.

Islamic Golden Age (750-1258)	
Capital moved to Bagdad.	

Abbasid Dynasty	
Second hereditary dynasty of Islam.	
750	Umayyuds fall to the Abbasids.
759	Abortive rebellion of mountain Lebanese against Abbasid rule after the harsh treatment of people living in Lebanese Syrian region.
	Fatimid Dynasty (909-1171)
	Ayyubid Dynasty (1171-1250)
936	Beit Maron and other Maronite monasteries completely destroyed during Christian persecution. 500 Maronite Christians martyred.
986	Beginning of the Druze religion and its expansion into several Lebanese regions.

Crusades 11th-13th Century	
Sanctioned by the Pope, the Crusades are a series of bloody, violent religious wars waged by Christians aimed at reclaiming Jerusalem and other holy sites in the Middle East from Muslim control. In all, 8 major Crusade expeditions occur, making Christians major players in the fight for land in the Middle East.	
1109	Crusaders take over Tripoli.

1200s: Mamluk Rule (1250-1516)	
Soldier-slave kings, known as Mumluks, overthrow the last Islamic dynasty the Ayyubids and rule Lebanon from the end of the 13th century for the best part of 300 years.	
1260	The county of Tripoli becomes a vassal state of the Mongol Empire

1268-1283	Mamluks attack strongholds of Maronites sowing destruction in Ehden, Becharre, Hadath El-Jibbet, Meifook, and other villages. Maronite Patriarch captured and killed.
1291	Shia Muslims and Druze in Lebanon rebel against the Mamluks who are fighting the European Crusaders and Mongols.

Ottoman Rule (1516-1918)

1516-17	Ottoman Sultan Selim I defeats the Mamluks.
1584	Pope Gregory XIII establishes Maronite Seminary in Rome.
8 May 1828	Maronite Catholic St Charbel born.
29 June 1832	St Rafqa – patroness of people in pain – is born.
Circa 1840	Conflict between the Druze and Maronite Christians leads to full scale war. Maronite revolt against the Feudal class lasts until 1858.
1842	Ottomans divide Mount Lebanon into two administrative regions, one Druze and the other Maronite Christian. Conflict between the two is encouraged by the Ottomans who practice a 'divide and rule' policy.
1860	**Mount Lebanon civil war** between Maronite Christian peasants and their Druze overlords. 20, 000 Christians killed and 380 Christian villages, and 560 churches destroyed. Napoleon III of France sends 7,000 troops to Beirut and helps impose a partition: Druze control of the territory is recognized as the fact on the ground and the Maronites are forced into an enclave. Arrangements ratified by the Concert of Europe in 1861.

1864	Under French pressure, The Ottoman Empire creates a semi-autonomous Christian territory in Mount Lebanon.
6th Dec 1883	Kahlil Gibran born in the village of Becharre, in the Cedars of Lebanon. Internationally renowned Lebanese poet, writer, artist and author of the beloved *"The Prophet"*.
1890	The "silk crisis". Cheaper and better quality Chinese silk and silk products flood Lebanon's main silk market: Europe. The crisis is especially hard as many had taken on large debt to expand their lands and plant mulberry trees – whose leaves were used to feed the worms.
24 Dec 1898	St Charbel dies.
Late 1800s –	Starting in the late 1800s and continuing into the early 1900s, **waves** of **Lebanese emigrate** to the Americas, Africa and Australia fleeing persecution and poverty.

Modern History: Post WWI

1914	St Rafqa dies
1914-1918	Ottomans block the roads to the mountains of Lebanon causing a human disaster. Tens of thousands of people die of famine and disease and thousands emigrate.
1920	Following the allied victory in WWI, France takes control of Lebanese territory and divides Lebanon and Syria into separate colonial enclaves/provinces – North Lebanon, South Lebanon, Bekaa and the State of Greater Lebanon – which includes Mount Lebanon.
1926	France declares the **Lebanese Republic**. It becomes a separate entity from Syria – but still administered under the French Mandate for Syria
10 April 1931	Kahlil Gibran dies

1932	National census held. Shows Maronite Christian community as largest sectarian group, followed by Sunni Muslims, Shia Muslims, Greek Orthodox and Druze.
1940	Lebanon comes under Vichy French control. General Henri Dentz plays a major role in the future independence of the nation.
1941	Turmoil in Europe sparks fears Germany will gain control of Syria and Lebanon, leading French and British troops to occupy Lebanon. After 20 years of French mandate, Lebanon's independence is declared in November, however full independence comes in stages.
Nov-Dec 1943	Free French forces imprison president Bechara El Khoury and other members of the Lebanese government after they declare an end to the French mandate. Following national and international pressure, they are released. The National Assembly is established on November 22, which is later known as **Independence Day.**
1 Jan 1944	France transfers power to the Lebanese government.
1945	World War II ends.
1948	The state of Israel is declared. Israel-Palestine war results in the exodus of thousands of Palestinians into Lebanon and Jordan.

First Civil War 1957-1958

1957-58	Muslims rally to pan-Arab call of Gamal Abdel Nasser, president of Egypt, and revolt against Maronite Christians. A short-lived civil war erupts. It is ended by the intervention of 5,000 US marines called in by President Carmille Chamoun according to the Eisenhower Doctrine, which offered US economic and military aid to countries in an effort to counteract Soviet global influence. This is known as "**Operation Blue Bat**", launched on 14 July.

5-10 June 1967	The **Six-day Arab Israeli War** between Israel and Arab nations Egypt, Syria and Jordan. Lebanon has no active role in the war but is affected as Palestinian factions use Lebanon as a base for retaliation strikes against Israel. Israel raids Beirut airport in retaliation for a Palestinian strike.
1973	Israel raid on Beirut kills three prominent Palestinian leaders associated with Palestine Liberation Organisation (PLO) Chairman Yasser Arafat. The Lebanese government resigns the next day.
	Lebanese Civil War (1975-1990)
13 April 1975	Right-wing Christian Phalangist gunmen ambush a bus in the Ain el-Rammaneh district of Beirut, killing 27 of its mainly Palestinian passengers. The Phalangists claim that guerrillas had previously attacked a church in the same district. This is widely considered to be the start of the lengthy civil war that devastated Lebanon.
1976	Fighting between Lebanese factions during March 1975 and November 1976 kills 40,000. Lebanon asks Syria to intervene to restore peace and curb the Palestinians. Syrian troops enter Lebanon. The Arab Summit arranges a ceasefire forming the Syrian Arab Deterrent Force (ADF) to maintain peace.
1978	Israel invades Southern Lebanon and occupies land reaching as far north as the Litani River. The United Nations Security Council calls on Israel to withdraw from Lebanese territory and creates a 6,000 man interim peacekeeping force called UNIFIL to ensure it happens. Israel hands over their strongholds to its proxy, the South Lebanon Army of mainly right-wing Christian Lebanese militia, instead of UNIFIL. Ehden Massacre. Phalangist gunmen attack the mansion of Frangieh family and murder Tony Frangieh, son of the

	Lebanese ex-President Sleiman Frangieh, his wife Vera, their three-year-old daughter Jihane, and thirty other Marada bodyguards and aides.
1983	A buffer zone is set up in south Lebanon. Israel and Lebanon sign an agreement on Israeli withdrawal. Suicide bombing of US embassy and US Marine barracks in 1983, which leave 258 Americans and 58 French servicemen dead, leads to multi-national Western peacekeeping forces withdrawal.
16 Feb 1985	Hezbollah (Party of God) is established Most Israeli troops withdraw, apart from the South Lebanon Army, some of whom remain along the South of the border and engage in clashes with Palestinian groups. Israel supports the Christian South Lebanon Army financed and trained by Israel and led by Major General Lahoud.
1986	Syria monitors a peacekeeping agreement in Beirut. Clashes between Shiite and Druze militia in West Beirut break the agreement. Syrian troops mobilize to suppress militia resistance.
1988	September 22 – Lebanese parliament fails to elect a successor to Amin Gemayel, Lebanon's prime minister. Gemayel appoints a six-member interim military government, comprising three Christians and three Muslims. Lebanon now has two governments – Salim al-Hoss heads the Muslim government in West Beirut while General Michel Aoun, the Maronite commander-in-chief of the Lebanese Army, controls East Beirut.
1989	The Taif peace agreement signed in Syria **ends the Civil War.** Muslims are given a greater voice in the political process.

1990-91	**Syrian Occupation.** Syrian air force attacks Presidential Palace at Baabda and overthrows President General Michel Aoun, who flees.
1991	Treaty of Brotherhood, Co-operation and Co-ordination is signed in Damascus by Lebanon and Syria, effectively giving Syria control over Lebanon's foreign relations. The Lebanese government, backed by Syria, regains control of the South and disbands various militia groups, ending the 16-year civil war which destroyed most of Lebanon's infrastructure. Israel withdraws from Lebanon. In August the national assembly grants amnesty for all crimes committed during the civil war. Aoun gets a presidential pardon and heads for exile in France.
1992	February 16 – Sheikh Abbas al-Musawi, Hezbollah's secretary-general, is killed when Israeli helicopter shoots at his motorcade near the town of Sidon. First elections since 1972. Nabih Berri, secretary-general of the Shiite Amal Party elected speaker of the national assembly, while Rafiq al-Hariri, a Saudi Arabian citizen and wealthy businessman with involvement in reconstruction and real estate, becomes prime minister. This is effectively a cabinet of technocrats – a technically/economically skilled elite.
11 -27 Apr 1996	"Operation Grapes of Wrath", Israel bombs Hezbollah bases in Southern Lebanon, Southern Beirut and the Bekaa Valley. UN base at Qana is hit, killing over 100 displaced civilians. Israel-Lebanon Monitoring Group, with members from US, France, Israel, Lebanon and Syria, set up to monitor truce.
1999	Israel bombs South Lebanon – the deadliest attack since 1996.

24 May 2000	Israel withdraws its forces from South Lebanon after the collapse of its proxy South Lebanon Army.
2005	**Syrian rule ends with the peaceful Cedar Revolution** of more than one million protesters in Beirut central district, following the assassination of the Lebanese PM Rafiq Hariri (14th Feb) and the withdrawal of the Syrian troops in April. Assassinations of anti-Syrian figures become a feature of political life. According to a NY times article in 2011: Outrage over the killing, which is widely blamed on Syria, leads to Syrian military withdrawal and a confrontation between two groups that will now wrestle for control of Lebanon. On one side is Hezbollah and its allies, backed by Syria and Iran; on the other a coalition allied to Saudi Arabia and the West, led by Hariri's son and heir, Saad Hariri.
2006	Israel attacks after Hezbollah kidnaps two Israeli soldiers. Civilian casualties are high and the damage to civilian infrastructure wide-ranging in 34-day war.
2007	Siege of Palestinian refugee camp Nahr al-Bared following clashes between Islamist militants and the Lebanese military. More than 300 people die and 40,000 residents flee before the army gains control of the camp.
Syrian Detente	
2008	May - Parliament elects army chief Michel Sleiman as president, ending six-month-long political deadlock. Sleiman re-reappoints Fouad Siniora as prime minister of national unity government. Lebanon establishes diplomatic relations with Syria for first time since both countries gained independence in 1940s.

2009[4]	International court to try suspected killers of former Prime Minister Hariri opens in Hague. Former Syrian intelligence officer Mohammed Zuhair al-Siddiq arrested in connection with killing. Four pro-Syrian Lebanese generals, held since 2005, freed after court rules there is not enough evidence to convict them.
Oct 2010	Hezbollah leader Hassan Nasrallah calls on Lebanon to boycott UN Hariri tribunal, saying it is "in league with Israel".
Jan 2011	Government collapses after Hezbollah and allied ministers resign.
2011	Beginning of conflict in Syria and **Syrian Civil War**
2011 June	Najib Mikati forms cabinet dominated by Hezbollah. UN's Special Tribunal for Lebanon issues four arrest warrants for the murder of Rafiq Hariri. The accused are members of Hezbollah, which says it won't allow their arrest.
Sept 2012	**Pope Benedict XVI's historic visit to Lebanon** on his "pilgrimage of peace for the entire region."
Oct 2012	Security chief Wissam al-Hassan is killed in car bombing. Opposition blames Syria.
Dec 2012	Syrian conflict spills into Lebanon in deadly clashes between Sunni Muslims and Alawites in Tripoli and Beirut. UN praises Lebanese families for taking in more than a third of the 160,000 Syrian refugees who have streamed into the country.
March 2013	Border tension: Syria fires rockets into northern Lebanon, days after Damascus warns Beirut to stop militants crossing the border to fight Syrian government forces.
2013	**Refugee Crisis**

[4] 2009-2017 information adapted from *BBC News 6 December 2017*

	The United Nations refugee agency says there are at least 700,000 Syrian refugees in Lebanon.
2013	Sharpening Sunni-Shia schism.
March 2013	Najib Mikati's government resigns amid tensions over upcoming elections.
April 2013	Sunni Muslim politician Tammam Salam is tasked with forming a new government.
May 2013	At least 10 people die in further sectarian clashes in Tripoli between supporters and opponents of the Syrian regime.
June 2013	A number of people are killed in clashes between Hezbollah gunmen and Syrian rebels within Lebanon.
July 2013	European Union lists the military wing of Hezbollah as a terrorist organization. This makes it illegal for Hezbollah sympathizers in Europe to send the group money, and enables the freezing of the group's assets there.
August 2013	Dozens killed in bomb attacks at two mosques in Tripoli. The twin attacks, which are linked to tensions over the Syrian conflict, are the deadliest in Lebanon since the end of the civil war in 1990.
Nov 2013	Double suicide bombing outside Iranian embassy in Beirut kills at least 22 people. It is one of the worst attacks in Shia southern Beirut since the conflict in Syria began.
Feb 2014	Sunni Muslim politician Tammam Salam finally assembles new power-sharing cabinet following 10 months of talks.
April 2014	UN announces the number of Syrian refugees registered in Lebanon has surpassed 1 million. One in every four people living in Lebanon is now a refugee from the Syrian conflict.
May 2014	President Sleiman ends his term of office, leaving a power vacuum. Several attempts are made over subsequent months to choose a successor.
August 2014	Syrian rebels overrun border town of Arsal. They withdraw after being challenged by the military but take 30 soldiers and police captive.

Sept 2014	Prime Minister Salam appeals to world leaders at the UN to help Lebanon face a "terrorist onslaught" and the flood of refugees from Syria.
Oct 2014	Clashes in Tripoli between the army and Islamist gunmen, in a spill-over of violence from the Syrian conflict.
Nov 2014	Parliament extends own term to 2017, citing Syria-related security concerns.
Jan 2015	Israel launches air strikes on Syrian side of the Golan, killing Hezbollah fighters and an Iranian general. Several clashes ensue across Israeli-Lebanese border. New restrictions on Syrians entering Lebanon come into effect, further slowing the flow of people trying to escape the war.
June 2016	Suicide bombings in Christian Al-Qaa, allegedly by Syrian nationals, aggravate already strained relations between Lebanese and the now more than 1 million Syrian refugees.
31 Oct 2016	Michel Aoun is elected president breaking a 29-month deadlock. He is a Maronite Christian and the founder of the Free Patriotic Movement.
July 2017	Hezbollah and Syrian army launch a military operation to dislodge Jihadist groups from the Arsal area, near the border with Syria.
Nov 2017	Prime Minister Hariri resigns, saying he senses a plot on his life. He withdraws his resignation a month later.

The Great Phoenician Period: 1550-300 BC

The area known today as Lebanon first appeared in recorded history around 3000 BC as part of a group of coastal cities colonized by the Phoenicians.

A seafaring people related to the Canaanites, the Phoenicians were one of the Mediterranean's greatest early civilizations.

They 'ruled the sea' and became the most notable traders and sailors of the ancient world. Their civilization thrived for more than a thousand years.

The fleets of the coastal city states travelled throughout the Mediterranean and even into the Atlantic Ocean, and other nations competed to employ Phoenician ships and crews in their navies.

These maritime geniuses founded many colonies, notably Utica and Carthage in North Africa, on the islands of Rhodes and Cyprus, the Iberian Peninsula and other Mediterranean areas. There is also recent archaeological evidence to suggest that the Phoenicians sailed as far as Celtic Britain.

The Phoenicians never unified politically: but they dominated as a result of enterprise and intellectual endeavour emanating from the coastal cities, each of which was an independent kingdom noted for the special activities of its inhabitants. Tyre and Sidon were important maritime and trade centres; Gubla (later known as Byblos and now as Jbeil) and Berytus (present-day Beirut) were trade and religious centres. Gubla was the first Phoenician city to trade actively with Egypt and the pharaohs of the Old Kingdom (2686-2181 BC), exporting cedar, olive oil, and wine, while importing gold and other products from the Nile Valley.

The most important Phoenician contribution to civilization was the alphabet. Purple dye, called Tyrian purple, the manufacture of textiles and the invention of glass, are also ascribed to the Phoenicians.

Phoenician cities were famous for their pantheistic religion. Each city had its special deity, usually known as its Baal, or Lord, and in all cities the temple was the centre of civil and social life. The most important Phoenician goddess was Astarte.

ABC of the Phoenicians

A - Alphabet's Creators

B - Builders of the first ships in history

C - Cadmus, the Father of Learning. Brother of Europa; taught the Greeks the alphabet, reputed founder of Thebes

D - Inventors of famous Tyrian purple dye

E - Europa, mythological mother of Europe and sister of Cadmus

F - Financial wizards and businessmen and women

G - Sailed in quest of silver, gold and trade

H - Home of the Cradle of Civilization

I - Inventors of glass making

J - Jewel of the Middle East

K – Kartaba (Qartaba), Phoenician village in Mount Lebanon

L - Their Land is Phoenicia = Lebanon

M - Melkart, Phoenician god of Tyre

N - Nautical Nation

O - One main god – Baal – served by the High Priest Melchizedek

P - Punic: Latin for Phoenician -world's first Empire on African soil

Q - Queen and goddess of the Phoenicians: Astarte

R - Rudiments of Polytheistic religions

S - First sailors to the Americas, before Columbus

T - Teachers of trade

U - First attempt at a united nations - Tripoli (The triple united polis or cities)

V - Vibrant

W - Berytus – Beirut - seat of the famous school of wisdom and law

X - Not xenophobic

Y - Yahweh's Temple of Solomon in Jerusalem built by the Phoenicians from Tyre

Z - Zarephath, a town in Phoenicia where the prophet Elijah met the widow

Modern Lebanon: Birth of the Lebanese Republic and the Beginning of Nation Building

To grasp just how significant a challenge and achievement it has been to create a Lebanese nation and an overarching ethos of *Lebanity* greater than the sum of its myriad and diverse religious and cultural parts, it helps to look briefly at the birth of the Lebanese Republic post World War I.

Prior to World War I, a separate state of Lebanon did not exist, but rather the Middle East comprised a tapestry of separate entities with different ethnicities, values, rulers and boundaries etc., under Ottoman Rule. It was the victorious allies – France and Britain – who, based on self-interest, political expediency and consideration of communications and access to oil, arbitrarily demarcated separate states in the Middle East (including the Jewish State of Israel in 1948, which was previously Palestine), effectively redrawing the map of the region.

Since 1861, the Maronite Christians had established a strong base in the mountains in 'Mount Lebanon' within the Ottoman system. It was on their insistence that the French agreed to extend the boundaries to include the Muslim coastal towns of Tyre, Tripoli, Beirut and Sidon, the fertile Bekaa Valley, Baalbek, Rashayya and Hasbayya into the independent state of 'Greater Lebanon' with Beirut as its capital.

The Maronites argued that 'Greater Lebanon' had always had a special social and historical character and boundaries. They upheld a unique history dating back to the ancient Phoenicians, which was distinct and exclusively theirs, different from their neighbours. They believed this made it imperative for France to help establish an independent state.

According to the eminent Lebanese historian Kamal Salibi, the Maronites were a strong united community with a long and proud tradition of mountain freedom and independence who spoke with one voice. They knew what they wanted, and so got it.

Consequently, in terms of the 1920 San Remo agreement between Britain and France, the latter was given a mandate over a territory extending from the Euphrates River to the Mediterranean coast.

The flag of this new Lebanon was none other than the French tricolour; with a cedar tree – now hailed as the glorious symbol of the ancient country since Biblical times – featured on the central white. Later, on 23 May 1926, the State of Greater Lebanon received a Constitution which transformed it into the Lebanese Republic.

Understandably the Muslim territories – with their own identity and aspirations – who were incorporated into Lebanon did not initially share the view that this was one coherent Nation.

So, it was from this cobbled together territory that the courageous, complex and difficult journey of true Nation building began, and the hospitable, warm hearted, richly diverse and colourful nation that we know today as Lebanon began to grow, and despite conflict and adversity, to flourish.

> *"To understand the heart and mind of a person, look not at what he has already achieved, but at what he aspires to."*
>
> *Kahlil Gibran, The Madman*

CHAPTER 3

Lebanon and Biblical History

The Golden Age of the Kings of Lebanon and Judah

*Those who honor me I will honor, and those who
despise me shall be treated with contempt.*
1 Samuel 2:30.

In Samuel, last of the great judges, we see the transition in Israel from
the period of the judges (military rulers) to the monarchy (kings).
Through the prophet, God rejects Saul (1 Samuel 15:10).
David is made king. His son is Solomon.
The second book of Samuel sees David reign, first as King over Judah
in the South (chapter 1-4) and then over the whole nation including
Israel in the North (5:24).
David struggles with his own people and his enemies.
David is also shown as being sometimes ruthless, and willing to commit
terrible sins to serve his own desires and ambitions.
But when he is confronted with his sins by the Lord's prophet, Nathan,
he repents.
David has a deep faith and a devotion to God Almighty. He wins the
loyalty of Hiram the Phoenician King of Tyre (980 to 943 BC).
King Hiram is treated as a brother by David and Solomon (1 Kings 5).
In this period, we have to look at the interaction of the spiritual life,
the political life and the economic or business life in the area.
In a nutshell business was in the hands of the Phoenicians, and spiritual
life was in the hands of the Israelites.
(There were no "Jews" at that time. The concept of Judaism only
developed after the return from exile in Babylon, 538 BC).

During the reign of King Hiram (37 years), the Canaanite kingdoms are independent.

Their merchant ships ply the Mediterranean Sea, using knowledge of the stars, wind and sea currents to navigate. Their aim is not military conquest, but trade.

Here are some of the primary gods of Canaan.

El – king of the gods.

Baal – son of El and god of fertility.

Mot – god of death and the underworld.

Anat – goddess of war and sacrifice.

Eshmun – god of Sidon, god of healing.

Melkart – god of Tyre.

But at the back of the minds of the Phoenicians, tucked away in the deep recesses, was the concept and hidden belief of the one true God of their brother Israelites.

In his book "The Hiram Code", Ron Phillips believes that God blessed the Phoenicians so they could take the alphabet, their ships and entrepreneurial skills to open the world. That at least two generations of Phoenicians believed in the concept of the 'One God'.

It is the action of the living God in the affairs of men. It is "Sacred History".

This period describes the origin of the worship of God in the Temple at Jerusalem, and especially the Levites.

DAVID: the real initiator of the temple in Jerusalem, 1010 – 970 BC.

SOLOMON: the architect, 970– 930 BC.

HIRAM: the builder. King of Phoenicia, 980 BC –to 947 BC.

Much was to happen during this period, as our story unfolds.

There is a warning and encouragement by God to be faithful to the covenant.

It is Temple and Worship.

It is a place of God.

It is the magnificence of their liturgy of sacrifice, prayer and praise in the building of the Temple.

But there are serious defects in the reign of King Solomon.

Solomon's Power

> *"Power corrupts, absolute power corrupts absolutely."* Anon.

King Solomon, the wisest, richest, most powerful king of all history, wants to fulfil his father's (King David) dream to build a Temple in Jerusalem to honour God Most High.

The principle interest is fidelity to Almighty God and his laws. In the fidelity of rulers. In the fidelity of people.

As the three Kings are good friends, Hiram is beckoned to build the Temple. The Lebanese have the skill, the workforce and are in close proximity. They get the job.

Hiram travels to Zimbabwe in Africa to get the Gold. Just a short distance from where the largest concentration of Lebanese on the African continent reside today – South Africa.

In 1 Kings 9-15 we see how King Solomon displeased the Lord in a number of ways: in payment to Hiram Solomon gives him wasteland in the region of Galilee. Hiram did not like the twenty villages, so they were called Cabul. He used forced labour to fill in the east side of the

City of Jerusalem and deprived the labourers of their wages, and he loved many foreign women.

The Prophets tell us that King Solomon would not be punished, but his offspring would.

930 BC sees the end of the Third Kingdom of Solomon.

The Song of Songs

I like to attend Holy Mass at the 'Church of Our Lady of the Cedars' in Wendywood, Johannesburg, South Africa.

The acoustics are good. I love the variety of people: Lebanese, African, visiting Christians from other parts of the world such as India, Iraq and Iran, Italian South Africans, Portuguese South Africans; a Lebanese Druze from the occupied territory of Palestine. Many others.

The anaphora (words of consecration of the Eucharist) is considered to be the most diverse in the Church, both Catholic and Orthodox.

I love the children and the vibe. How lovely when at communion time they go to the altar and receive the blessing. The Priest or Deacon placing the chalice of the Lord on their heads.

The words of consecration in the language spoken by Jesus – Aramaic. The delightful music in English, Arabic and Aramaic.

The fellowship after Mass and naturally the Lebanese bread and delicacies on offer after mass.

Now my story: The "Song of Songs" means the greatest of songs. The Song of Solomon.

As you enter the Church above the main altar is a round stained glass window – donated by the owner of the firm Nicolo Giuricich and family. It depicts the coronation of the Blessed Virgin Mary as Queen of Heaven:

This representation has profound historical significance for Maronites as it is based on a drawing taken from one of the old extant (still existing) illuminated frescos (a picture painted on a wall before the plaster is dry) in the Qadisha Valley, North Lebanon. It exists in the old monastery of Our Lady of Qannoubine.

This window is designed by Joan Blunden, a South African artist.
It is framed by a locally fabricated terrazzo surround, and is emblazoned in Arabic and English with the Motif:

Come with me from Lebanon, my bride;
come with me from Lebanon.
Bible: Song of Songs 4:8.

In the book of Revelation 19:7 we read:

"... for the marriage of the Lamb has come,
and his bride has made herself ready"

The "Song of Songs" is a beautiful love song. Dedicated to King Solomon, it is a pure love song between a man and a woman. It is about the purity of marriage. The way Almighty God wishes it to be. It is not the love of lust or illicit sex.

It is written in Aramaic, the language of the Lebanese of that epoch. Solomon had many wives, so he spoke many languages of that area.

We in South Africa can relate to this because of our eleven official languages.
We can also relate to all the wives of the mighty King Solomon, many of them Phoenician. Some commentators even say his favourite wife was Phoenician and not Egyptian.

The "Song of Songs" has often been interpreted by the Jewish People as a picture of the relationship between God and his People, and by the "People of the Cedars" – the Lebanese People – as a relationship between Our Lord Jesus Christ and the Church: Jesus the Bridegroom, and the Bride from Lebanon, the Church.

Judaism in Preparation for the Coming of Jesus (586 BC to AD 1)

Following the conquest of the Northern Kingdom by the Assyrians in 721/2 BC the 10 tribes of Israel disperse and are gradually assimilated into the Canaanite communities and thus disappear from history. Only the line of David is retained.

Canaanites are identified in Genesis of the Bible as descendants of Canaan, a son of Ham and grandson of Noah. Canaan was all of present day Palestine, Lebanon and Syria.

As there were no planes, cars, or helicopters, the only means of transport was by foot – Shank's pony, by "Da donkey" and for the more privileged, by horse. Contrary to popular belief, there are no camels in

Lebanon. Lebanon, as always, was the best destination, and absorbed the majority of the ten tribes of Israel. In Biblical times, people could walk 32 km in one day.

The first destruction of the Temple (by the Babylonians) occurs in 586 BC and led to the exile of the Israelites.

The book of Lamentations states that Ezekiel (593-571) is the first Jewish prophet in Babylon and in exile. The vicissitudes under various rulers and the calling of the Jewish people are described by the Prophets Haggai, Zechariah, Ezra, Nehemiah and Malachi in the Bible.

In 558 BC the Jewish people lived under favourable conditions.

538 BC: Return of the Israelites from exile in Babylon. Now known as Jews.

In 350 BC, the Jewish people enjoy a liberal policy under Persian overlords.

In 334 BC the Samaritan Community – a small sect originating from the Israelites – exert a liberating influence on all neighbours. This is in sharp contrast with the narrow restricted Judaism centred in Jerusalem.

By 332 BC Judah and the near East – including Phoenicia – is under the rule of Alexander the Great who brought with him the Greek culture and language – leading to a co-mingling of Hellenism and Judaism. The Jewish people still worship the God of their fathers, but speak Greek.

In 275 BC the Old Testament is translated from Hebrew into Greek. Between 247 BC and 222 BC the Egyptians under Ptolemy III trample the Jewish people in Palestine.

In 198 BC we see the final power of Syria in Palestine.

167 BC the Maccabean Revolt is followed by friendly relations with Rome from 143 BC to 135 BC.

Around 110 BC we see the introduction of the Pharisees, the Sadducees and the Essenes. The Essenes are a Jewish sect, who consider themselves to be a separate people, because of the illumination of their inner lives.

They felt that they had been entrusted with a special mission, which would lead to Christianity. They would change the world, and the course of history. Saint Ann, Saint Joachim, Joseph and Mary, John the Baptist and John the Evangelist were all Essenes.

Our God Almighty chose these people to allow the Holy Spirit to conceive Our Blessed Lady immaculately.

It was the Holy Spirit, as father, so all humanity is included. It was the Jewish people who were privileged, because they were the only people who believed in the concept of one God.

The line of David in Mary, was all embracing. Ruth, the Moabite woman, Rahab, the woman of ill repute and many Semitic women are represented.

It was in Phoenicia, Lebanon that the populace first embraced Jesus and Christianity.

There are fourteen Generations from the return of the Israelites from Babylon to the coming of Jesus.

We, the Lebanese in South Africa, can understand this timeline as we have been of Africa, and in Africa, for over 125 years.

Jesus's Lebanese Ethos

In my book "People of the Cedars: A 20th Century Insight into the Lebanese South African Community" I mention that:

- The High priest, the King of Salem blessed Abram in the name of God Most High in Canaan – site of present day Lebanon (Genesis 14:19).
- Abraham, the father of many nations was a wandering Aramaean and father of present day Christians, Jews and Muslims – the three great Monotheistic religions. If he came and settled in this area today Abraham would be an Iraqi Lebanese. Just as the Armenians of today are Armenian Lebanese.
- The Phoenicians (modern day Lebanese) named Britain and Europe, and that Cadmus was the Father of Learning.
- The Phoenicians invented the Alphabet. They sailed to America and circumnavigated Africa over 2000 years before the Europeans.
- Lebanon was part of the cradle of our modern civilization.
- The Cedar Tree of Lebanon is named after God and dedicated to Him.
- Certain Lebanese scholars and other theologians believe that the Transfiguration of Jesus took place in the Holy Cedars of Lebanon.

Is Jesus Lebanese?

If you do not believe in the Bible, then there is no argument. No discussion.

We then talk about the weather, sport, Manchester United, drink beer and eat boerewors (a traditional South African sausage). We go to the horse races and rugby. Work our guts out. Come home, eat and watch television and go to sleep, to confront hectic traffic the next morning.

This is what C.S. Lewis said about Christianity:

> *Christianity, if false, is of no importance, and if true, of infinite importance. The only thing it cannot be is moderately important."*

If you do believe in the Bible, then you believe:

-That Jesus is the second person of the Blessed Trinity.

-That many of the women in the line of Mary were Phoenician.

-That Ruth was a Moabite woman. That there was even a woman of ill repute: Rahab (Matthew 1:5). A gentile woman of faith.

-That our Lord Jesus Christ spoke Aramaic, the language of the Lebanese 2000 years ago. He walked preached and identified himself with the people of Sidon and Tyre.

-That his first miracle, turning water into wine, was in Cana, South Lebanon.

-That he formed the Church at Caesarea Philippi in the foothills of Mount Hermon to get away from those who wished Him harm.

-With the Miracle of the Loaves and the Fishes, Jesus did not make a profit.

-Jesus's ethos was certainly Lebanese.

> ## "Lebanon portrays the heart that pumps the blood of life to the whole world"
>
> *President of Lebanon H.E. General Michel Aoun*

Lebanon in the New Testament

The Transfiguration

Meaning and significance of the Transfiguration

Before his crucifixion and resurrection, Jesus was in Galilee. He was met by a group of Pharisees and Sadducees – two conflicting religious, cultural and political Jewish groups.

The Pharisees were adherents to oral laws and traditions, and believed in an afterlife and the coming of a Messiah. They had the support and goodwill of the common people

The Sadducees were the more elite upper class, who represented the authority of the priestly privileges, and did not believe in an afterlife.

Both were opposed to Jesus. The Pharisees because he wasn't observing all the purity laws (e.g. he associated with tax collectors and prostitutes) and the Sadducees because they feared the reactions of the Romans.

Lebanon's Water and the Baptism of Jesus

Lebanon's waters flow from the mountains when the snow melts. They flow into the Jordan River. And to the oceans and the whole world.

"And a voice came from heaven which said: "You are my beloved Son; with you I am well pleased" Luke 3:22.

Jesus had come to Saint John the Baptist to be baptised to epitomize all to which the Mosaic Law pointed; and all that the Prophets had foretold

Therefore, Jesus decided to leave the region of Galilee. He set out North West towards the mountains where the Transfiguration was to take place.

He moved to Caesarea Philippi, about 50 km north of the Sea of Galilee. Here he formed the Church. Peter acknowledged Jesus as the Messiah. Peter is the rock on which the Church is built.

Six to eight days later, after these happenings, the Transfiguration occurred.

Jesus took with him Peter, James and John and led them up a high mountain where they were alone. A change came over Jesus: His face was shining like the sun, and His clothes were dazzling white. Then the three disciples saw Moses and Elijah talking to Jesus. (Matthew 17:1-4; Mark 9:2-4 and Luke 9:28-36).

A voice said from the cloud, "This is my Son, my Chosen; listen to him!" (Luke 9:35).

According to Catholic Saint and Scholar, Thomas Aquinas, the Transfiguration was the greatest miracle in that it complemented Baptism and showed the perfection of life in Heaven.

This is what happened at the Transfiguration

Holiness was brought to perfection in our Lord Jesus, son of David and the promised Messiah.

The Prophecies of the Old Testament were brought to fulfilment in Jesus.

The Holy Spirit of God Almighty was present.

The Divine and earthly were united in Jesus, the Son of Man and Son of God.

Elijah represented the Prophets of the Old Testament.
Moses represented the Ten Commandments and the Law.
Peter, James and John and the Disciples represented the "People of God".
All were placed in the Arms of Jesus the Christ.

The transfiguration took place on the way to Christ's trial, conviction, crucifixion, death and resurrection.

Church of the Transfiguration in the Forests of the Cedars of Lebanon. The Transfiguration of Christ possibly took place near here.[5]

[5] Photo courtesy "History of the Maronites : Religious, Cultural and Political". Rev Butros Dau, 1984

An Argument for the Transfiguration taking place in the Holy Cedars of Lebanon

There are three mountains contending for the place of the Transfiguration: Mount Tabor, Mount Hermon and The Holy Cedars of Lebanon. As a Lebanese, I am rooting for The Holy Cedars of Lebanon.

In his book "Religious, Cultural, and Political History of the Maronites", Rev. Butros Dau, makes a compelling argument for the Transfiguration taking place in the Holy Cedars of Lebanon. According to him there are six criteria the Mountain has to meet:

It is a Holy Mountain
Peter in the second Epistle 1:16-18 says "We ourselves heard this voice come from heaven, while we were with him on the holy mountain". The expression "The Holy Mountain" is the title the Bible and literature of the oriental peoples have given to Lebanon alone, from ancient times to the present day. Lebanon, and especially the Northern part where the Cedars are, is called by Ezekiel "The Holy Mountain of God". (Ezekiel 28: 14-17).

It is a High Mountain
In Luke 9:37 we read that it took a whole day to come down the mountain. The Cedars of Lebanon are high: 3000 meters above sea level. Ten to twelve hours are required to come down from it. In contrast Mount Tabor is not a high mountain, rising only 562 meters above sea level

It is six to eight days' journey on foot from Caesarea Philippi
It takes six days to walk from Caesarea Philippi to the Cedars of Lebanon, which suggests that the time was spent travelling towards the Mountain of Transfiguration.

It is a lonely Mountain

It must be out of the reach of Herod, the Pharisees and the Sadducees and all those who wished our Beloved Jesus harm, as they thought of Him as a revolutionary.

It is outside of Galilee

It is North of Capernaum.

It is certified by ancient and serious tradition as the place of the Transfiguration

The Holy Cedars of Lebanon meet all of these criteria.

The languages of Moses, Jesus and the Lebanese

According to the Bible, after his mother hid him in a basket and sent him down the Nile to save him from being murdered by the Pharaoh of Egypt, Moses was fortuitously found and adopted by Pharaoh's daughter. So undoubtedly he grew up speaking Egyptian.

Egyptian is the oldest known language of Egypt – and one of the oldest recorded languages. The earliest complete sentence dates to about 2690 BC. This was 900 years before the Israelites entered Egypt. Jacob (Israel) and the 70 who entered Egypt were descendants of the wandering Aramaean Abraham – Father of many Nations. Their language was Aramaic.

The Israelites mingled with the native tribes in Egypt and became a nation. They were in Egypt from approx. 1700 to 1250 BC. We can assume that they had lost their original Semitic Aramaic language after 450 years in bondage, and that the 600,000 men, besides women and children, that Moses led out of Egypt in the Exodus, spoke Egyptian.

Egyptian is part of the large family of Afro-Asiatic languages – those from both Africa and the Middle East. Today Afro-Asiatic languages comprise around 375 genetically related languages and dialects spoken in Africa, the Middle East and the Arabian Peninsula.

The most widely spoken of these is Arabic. A language within the Semitic branch of the Afro-Asiatic languages, it includes 35 varieties – Modern Standard Arabic as well as spoken colloquial Arabic. Lebanese Arabic is one such version.

The Egyptian that Moses spoke is now extinct. The Lebanese (descendants of the Phoenicians and the Aramaean) in South Africa can relate to losing a language.

Sadly, after only around 125 years (2018) in the country, we have (largely) lost the language of our ancestors. The language of the Holy Land. The majority today speak English.

There is however a resurgence of interest among young people who wish to preserve the language of their ancestors and learn Arabic. I still speak the tongue of my mother and have initiated and co-taught classes in Arabic in Johannesburg.

Until recently Holy Mass in our Maronite Catholic churches was conducted in Syriac – a liturgical dialect of Aramaic – the language of Moses and the one that historians agree was spoken by Jesus and his disciples.

Although Greek and Hebrew were also spoken, Aramaic was the common language of Judea in the first century AD. The words of consecration of the Eucharist during Holy Mass are still spoken in Aramaic today.

CHAPTER 4

Lebanese Luminaries

Of the countless commendable Lebanese entrepreneurs, religious, professionals, sports and business men and women and philanthropists in South Africa and around the world, I have chosen to highlight the lives of several people who exemplify the qualities of generous and selfless dedication to their culture and community, and success and vision.

Lebanon's African Hero: Roy Hanna

In Memoriam: Beloved cousin and friend

25 January 1939 – 3rd September 2017

When Roy was born into a Lebanese South African family little did anyone realize that his life was to be one of great significance and meaning, nor that he would touch people with his great stature, wisdom, business genius, integrity, sportsmanship and love of people.

At school he excelled at sport and was dubbed "The Rugby Player". He played for Parktown Boys High first team, going on to first league rugby and Provincial under 21 honours.

Family life

At the tender age of 21 Roy married Thora Peter then aged 19. They were married for 57 years.

> *"A virtuous woman is a crown to her husband."*
> *"Whoso findeth a wife findeth a good thing, and*
> *obtaineth favour of the Lord". Proverbs 12:4 and*
> *18:22; King James Bible.*

Roy and Thora

The marriage produced five children, ten grandchildren and one great grandchild. All Roy's grandchildren have excelled in sport at school, national and international level. For example, after Roy's funeral his grandson Jordan was off to Italy to play professional rugby. But Roy insisted that they also obtain an university education as he believed they could not rely on sport as they got older. They have heeded their Jidu's advice.

Roy took his family of 21 on two world tours to Europe and the Caribbean, and has homes on the Vaal River and in San Lameer on the Natal South Coast.

Entrepreneur

Roy grew to become an outstanding entrepreneur and businessman. His timing was perfect, as when he captured the video industry at its peak, opening over 200 outlets throughout South Africa and Africa. Later he diversified into real estate and the stock market.

His family became the backbone of his business empire. A family that prays together, stays together. Roy and Thora prayed every Thursday together and read the Bible as a family. Says daughter Lynne, "We work very hard to keep the family united and love our great Sunday get togethers and luncheons".

Roy and his faith

The ability to implement an idea is as important as the idea itself.

Roy's cousin, Pete Samra, an evangelical pastor in the USA, had a vision and a calling to build churches throughout South Africa. "Change the Townships, change the Cities" is Pete's motto. Roy responded generously to the call and financed the building of 39 churches.

"God's fire over Africa" Conference was held in Johannesburg in 2016 and catered for Pastors in South Africa and other parts of Africa. In May 2017, just before being hospitalized, Roy spoke to Pastors and encouraged them with his foresight and entrepreneurial wisdom.

Roy remained a Maronite. At his funeral service the Pastor at Liberty Church, Mark Reeves, introduced Father Maurice Chidiac, Head of the Lebanese Maronite Mission in South Africa to great applause from the almost 700 mourners who came to celebrate the life and times of Brother Roy.

With the playing of the 'The Lord's Prayer' in Lebanese, Roy's life and the presence of the two Ministers – one Catholic, one Protestant – a perfect example of ecumenism in the Christian communion was portrayed.

When the "Holy Spirit" led the Pastor to bless the ten grandchildren, we witnessed something that was very beautiful, very special. From above.

Community Contribution

His charitable works knew no bounds.

Roy tithed generously and supported many families. Nobody was turned away when financial help was needed. The more he gave, the more he got.

For 47 years Roy encouraged and helped finance the Lebanese newspaper, the "Cedar Leaf" serving the Lebanese South African Community, which I edited. With Roy's financial help I was able to serve Lebanese families in South Africa and abroad. He also helped finance my first book "People of the Cedars: A 20th Century Insight into the Lebanese South African Community".

Roy was also a prime benefactor in the building of the Shrine to Our Lady, at the Lebanese Maronite Church of Our Lady of Lebanon in Mulbarton, Johannesburg.

He was the Treasurer of the South African Lebanese Association, under Joe Lebos and supported the Cedar Park Country Club. He loved Fred Tarry, Cedar Park hero of yesteryear. Roy encouraged the community to get the Club into the hands of the Church for posterity. During Roy's lifetime the community grew from strength to strength.

Roy and Lebanon

Roy loved Lebanon, and ensured that his family obtained Lebanese citizenship. He especially loved Becharre, our family's ancestral village, and helped finance the building of a Memorial to our Jidu (grandfather) and Situ (grandmother) which stands proudly in the Holy Cedars. He also financed levelling the ground for future generations to build a family home in the mountains of Lebanon.

World Lebanese Cultural Union WLCU

When the WLCU visited South Africa on a number of occasions, Roy financed their costs and supplied transport for the delegates.

Horse Racing

Roy loved the lure of the gamble and the majesty of the horse and at the time of his death he owned more than 25 race horses. He considered Mark Tarry to be the best breeder in the country and brother Sean Tarry the best trainer in South Africa

Roy features prominently in the books written on the Lebanese Community. Roy loved King Solomon of the Old Testament. These words aptly apply to Roy's life.

> *"I have fought the good fight, I have finished the race, I have kept the faith. From now on there is reserved for me the crown of righteousness." (2 Timothy 4:7-8).*

Lebanon's Canadian Titan: Dr Nick Kahwaji

They have gone and the world commemorates the disaster without mentioning them.

125 Lebanese emigrants lost their lives, and 29 survived the sinking of the "unsinkable" liner.

They are the men and women of the historical and holy land of Lebanon who would be remembered as heroes of the Titanic disaster.

The Titanic in 1912 was the world's largest liner. It was on a maiden voyage from Southampton in England to New York in America.
Her passengers were a cross section of Edwardian Society, from millionaires to poor emigrants seeking a new life in America.

The ship sailed on 14th April 1912. There were 1320 passengers on board and 892 crew members. The Lebanese accounted for just less than 10% of the passengers – mainly in 3rd class.

Between the 14th and 15th April 1912, the Titanic hit an iceberg which cut into the starboard side, creating the greatest disaster in shipping history. Films have been produced and the world community is aware and shocked at this disaster. But the Lebanese are never mentioned.

Someone has set out to change that. Dr Nick Kahwaji is a Lebanese Canadian. He is a member of the World Lebanese Cultural Union (WLCU), an organization representative of the Lebanese Diaspora throughout the world. The Union was founded over 58 years ago with total commitment to the Lebanese abroad.

As the President of the WLCU British Columbia Council in Canada, Nick stood for office and became the Secretary General of the World organization.

He is also the chief executive of the "International Phoenician Research Centre Inc."

Nick saw the necessity of honouring the Lebanese aboard the Titanic, and in 2012 (the centennial of the Titanic's tragic sinking) the International Lebanese Titanic Committee (ILTC) was established.
Together with the Lebanese Emigration Research Center (LERC) and the Irish-Lebanese Cultural Foundation (ILCF), Nick asked the simple questions: How many Lebanese were on board? How many survived? How did they die? Where did they come from?
The word Titanic means huge, epic, or enormous. The idea has grown exponentially.

The Lebanon and Migration Nucleus Museum at Notre Dame University in Beirut (LMM) has an authentic scale replica of the Titanic. The plaque lists the names of the Lebanese who were on board, and those who perished in the tragedy.

One of the survivors is Shaanineh abi Raad. Her story is very touching, and one most Lebanese descendants in the Diaspora can relate to, as it reflects the plight of most of our ancestors.

People in the mountains of Lebanon were struggling to make a living. Emigration was the only answer, so 38 year old Shaanineh set out from her native village of Thoum by donkey to Beirut. Then by boat to Marseille, train to Gare St Lazare in Paris, an arduous six hour train ride to Cherbourg in Northern France and then onto the Titanic and on her way to her family in Youngstown Ohio.

Shaanineh was rescued on the famous Titanic's Collapsible C, but sadly her four male cousins with whom she was travelling, drowned. On reaching America *The Hebrew Immigrant Aid Society* (HIAS) provided her with food, clothing and shelter and $50 for a train ticket to her home in Youngstown where she tirelessly laboured by peddling and doing domestic work to support her family. She later moved to Sharon, Pennsylvania where her family opened a grocery store. Her children Rose and Albert launched the Thomas Ice Cream Cone Company, which later became renowned as the Joy Cone Company of Hermitage, Pennsylvania. Today, the Joy Cone Company is the largest ice cream cone company in the world, baking over 1.5 billion cones/year.

The fruits of her courage, hardship, resilience and determination continue to echo in the current migration from Lebanon.

This determination of the Lebanese abroad the Titanic was expressed in a joint painting exhibition prepared by Dr Nick Kahwaji, Dr Guita Hourani and Artist Bernard Renno during the Lebanese Diaspora Energy (LDE) conference in Beirut 2016 and included 29 painters and artists.

Following this exhibition, the artists donated their work to the LMM. One was selected by H.E. Minister Gebran Bassil to be exhibited at the Emigrant Museum in Batroun.

We salute Nick for unveiling this story, but not without a final word. Out of a torn country (Lebanon) to peace (Canada) is the 24-year family history of Nick's struggle.

Age 51 he is married, is father to four children and runs a successful Dental Practice in British Columbia.

He is the Editor of the "Lebanese Heritage".

He is also working with H.E. Wadih Fares (Lebanese honorary council in Halifax):
- To commemorate the Lebanese who died abroad the Titanic by installing a commemorative plaque and planting a Lebanese cedar tree in a park in Halifax.

- To finalize renovation of the Lebanese Canadian Diaspora House in Batroun.

- In British Columbia he is working with the WLCU-BC council on installing the Lebanese Emigrant Statue in the centennial Park in Victoria.

According to Dr Nick Kahwaji, the World needs Lebanese affection and Canadian standards.

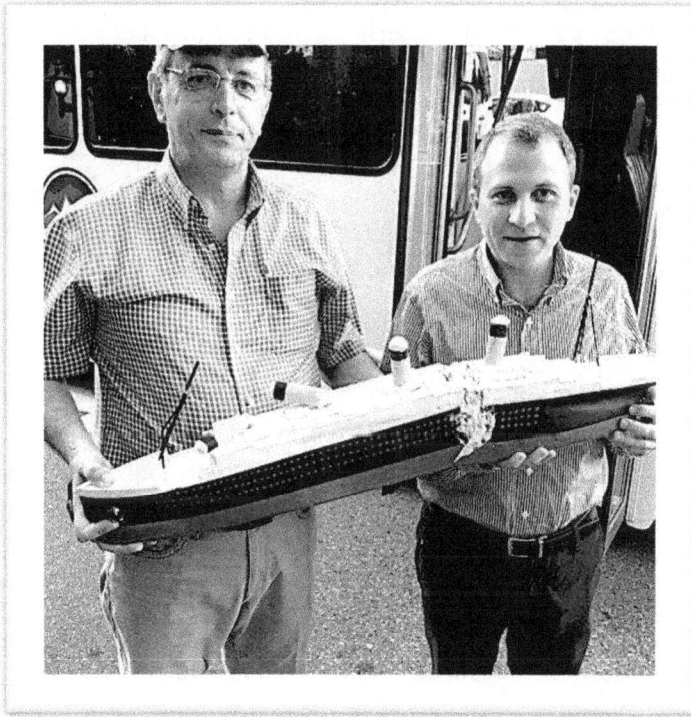

Nick Kahwaji (left) and Lebanese Minister of Foreign Affairs, H.E. Gebran Bassil with a model of the *Titanic*

Market Magic: Dr Azar Jammine

Have you ever asked the question: what is an economist and what does she or he do? Let's take a look at one of South Africa's leading economists, Dr Azar Jammine.

Azar is son of a doyen of the Lebanese Community of yesteryear, the eminent sociologist Dr Emile Jammine, who was instrumental in advancing the World Lebanese Cultural Union in South Africa (WLCU) – a movement which he led with distinction during the 1970's. Emile's ancestral village is Zgharta in North Lebanon. He was a Maronite and his wife Greek Orthodox.

Azar is married to Georgia, a speech therapist of Greek descent. The couple has two children, daughter Aida Catherine (named after her paternal Situ), and son Jean-Emile (named after both his maternal and paternal grandfathers), and three grandchildren.

Azar regrets that his children never knew their grandparents as they were either too small or not born when their grandparents died.

The couple practice their faith in the Greek Orthodox tradition. It is interesting to note that Maronite Catholics are permitted to take Holy Communion in the Orthodox Church, and vice versa.

Azar's Lebanese connections are impressive. The President of the Republic of Lebanon during the 1970's was his uncle H.E. Sleiman Franjieh. Azar's mom and Franjieh's wife, Iris, were sisters. Azar spent much time in North Lebanon during the Franjieh term of office.

Ehden, near the immortal Cedars of Lebanon, is the home village of the Franjieh clan. Both President Franjieh and his son Tony were Maronites, but married Greek Orthodox wives.

As for Azar's profession, in laymen's terms it appears that it is all about selective data which is entered into computers to produce market moving analyses which are used by the corporate world and governments in helping to make decisions which amount to millions of Rand each day. It involves money, markets and the economist's magic.

This is basically how Azar, a London School of Economics graduate with a PhD degree in economics, earns his living.

The simplest form of economics is in the home. A prudent family economizes; spends less than what they earn. "Spend one cent more than you earn = disaster. Spend one cent less than you earn = success". These same principles apply to the corporate world and governments – Azar's clients.

To economize is to use sparingly, to save and practice thrift. It is the careful and judicious management of money and embraces frugality and correct decisions and utilization of labour, time and resources.

Dr Jammine is Chief Economist of the highly respected economic consultancy 'Econometrix' in Houghton, Johannesburg – just up the road from Madiba's (Nelson Mandela) residence and centre. He always – well almost always – gets his analysis right.

With the economic information that his consultancy generates on a daily basis, they can possibly influence the way the macro and micro economy of the country performs.

With Azar's qualifications and expertise, he could have gone anywhere in the world. He chose South Africa as his home. It is our community – and South Africa's – gain.

Dr Azar Jammine- Lebanon's African Economist

Dr Jammine matriculated at Pretoria Boys' High School after which he completed a BSc Honours in Mathematical Statistics at the University of the Witwatersrand.

He represented Wits and Transvaal under 20 at rugby.

Between 1970 and 75 he was employed as Investment Analyst at Senbank and subsequently at stockbrokers Martin & Co, now JP

Morgan, during which time he completed a B.A. Honours in Economics, cum laude, part-time at Wits.

In 1976 Dr Jammine completed his M.Sc. in Economics at the London School of Economics, followed by his PhD at the London Business School after which he was awarded a two-year Post-Doctoral Fellowship at the Centre for Business Strategy of the School.

In order to pay his way whilst working on his PhD, Dr Jammine used his knowledge of six languages to conduct international business consultancy projects in Europe, North America and the Far East, covering a wide variety of industries.

Dr Jammine returned to South Africa in 1985 to become Director and Chief Economist of Econometrix (Pty) Limited, a position he has occupied ever since.

Dr Jammine has published articles in international strategic management journals and is co-author of *"McGregor's Economic Alternatives"*, *"Trends Transforming South Africa"* and *"Mindset for the New Generation on South Africa"*, all published by Juta.

His contribution to *McGregor's Economic Alternatives* was used by the ANC in the organisation's internal training programme.

He has conducted thousands of presentations at conferences globally on local and international economics, has been quoted in over 1,500 newspaper and magazine articles in South Africa and abroad, and has been interviewed hundreds of times in local and international media.

Lebanon's Paris Patriarch: Antoine Menassa

The dynamic Antoine Menassa who has helped promote the uniqueness of the Lebanese Diaspora – is the son of the Qadisha valley region of Lebanon. The Holy Valley. The valley of saints and poets throughout the ages.

He harmoniously blends the contemplativeness of the saints and the great imagination of the poets, and absorbs these into his economic philosophy. He ignites a new passion for Lebanon. "Good business makes good friends" is an appropriate quotation.

"He who loves Lebanon most will love and serve France first". These are the words of the great Lebanese philosopher and thinker Dr Charles Malik.

This love affair between Lebanon and France goes way back to the Crusaders in the 11th century.

Antoine is the Chairperson of the Business and Economic Committee of the World Lebanese Cultural Union (WLCU). He is also president of the French Lebanese Business Association.

He strongly advocates that Lebanese expats should stay away from political wrangling. This is vital for the economic role the Diaspora is playing, and will play in the future.

"Lebanon's survival depends on sound financial principles," says Antoine.

Antoine's ancestry

Antoine's father Chekrallah Gergios Menassa was from Tyre, South Lebanon. In the 1930s he joined his sister Rose (married to Gebran Wakim) in Dakar, Senegal where he founded the largest cardboard suitcase manufacturing business in West Africa – producing 2,000 suitcases a day.

In 1948 he returned to Lebanon to find a wife. After visiting numerous families it was Marie Torbey who won his heart. Within 15 days the two were married and set off to honeymoon in Beirut, before returning to Senegal where Antoine was born in 1949.

When political troubles began after independence in 1961, Antoine (12) and his brother were sent to school in Lebanon to learn Lebanese (at that time he could only speak French – but is now tri-lingual).

It was during this time that he grew a deep love for North Lebanon and the Holy Qadisha Valley.

Antoine's parents and twin sisters joined him in Lebanon when he was 17 and the family settled in Tripoli – which he describes as a 'paradise'.

His career in finance began modestly – stamping 500 envelopes on his first day at a job in a bank. But he persevered – working in the mornings at the bank, teaching at a girls' school and travelling 100 km every two days to St Joseph's University to study for his Diploma in Banking Administration and Management, which he completed in 1974.

Antoine rose up the ranks in his profession – eventually growing a large, successful bank in France – where he has lived for the past 43 years, travelling happily between there and Lebanon.

Antoine married his wife Adela – daughter of Don Jose Harfuch, from a large Mexican family – in 1986. As a consequence of this rich history, the couple's son Antoine Chekrallah is tri-national: French, Lebanese and Mexican.

Antoine and the Lebanese Diaspora Energy Conference (LDE)

During May of 2017 the Lebanese Diaspora Energy (LDE) conference was held in Beirut.

One of the discussion panels was the Diaspora Economic Forum. The theme: "A Dialogue with Dreamers". The 15 panellists included H.E. Raed Khoury, Minister of Economy and Trade, Lebanon; H.E. Monie Captan, former Minister of Foreign affairs, Liberia; Mr Faddy Zouky, President of the Lebanese Australian Chamber of Commerce in Melbourne. Other countries represented were Brazil, Côte d'Ivoire, Canada, Mexico, Saudi Arabia, and the Sultanate of Muscat and Oman. The main objective of this sector was economic unity of purpose.

Issues that were discussed included networking which takes into consideration the uniqueness of the Lebanese Diaspora, reactivating the Ministry of Foreign Affairs and Emigrants' role via their ambassadors when communicating with foreign authorities in backing Lebanese businessmen and businesses.

Main objectives of networking:

- Provide a platform to inform and channel the influence of Lebanese economic executives worldwide
- Provide reliable data and consistent information on existing business opportunities for the Lebanese Diaspora to ensure better co-operation.
- Contribute to the amelioration and development of the Lebanese economy, and create strong bonds between business people in Lebanon and the Diaspora.

There are numerous benefits of this network, including the creation of a community designed to facilitate exchange, and share information, talents and expertise.

Antoine Menassa, we believe, encapsulates all that is noble in the initiative. He has visited Lebanese communities throughout the world and Lebanon, including Australia and South Africa, where his dedication endeared him to the Lebanese community. A powerful man, who showed both humility and love.

In a letter to Antoine, Mrs Dona Turk, Director of Economic Affairs of the Ministry of Foreign Affairs, Lebanon thanked him for his passion and commitment to Lebanon and its shared economic journey.

Antoine is involved in the rapidly growing Fintech (Financial Technology) hub, where innovative technology is enhancing and expanding the delivery of financial services.

Uruguay Connect: José María Almada Sad

José (left) with former Lebanese President H.E. Michel Sleiman

Tucked away snugly in the South Eastern region of South America is the country of Uruguay.

It borders Argentina to the West and Brazil to the North and East, with the Rio de la Plata (River of Silver) to the South and the Atlantic Ocean to the South East.

Of a total population of over 3 million, there are approximately 70,000 of Lebanese descent comprising one of the largest non-European communities in Uruguay. Vice President Alberto Abdalla (1968 to 1972) was also Lebanese.

Uruguay also boasts another Lebanese hero, José María Almada Sad, who since 2008 has single-handedly produced a News Magazine for the

Lebanese community in Uruguay called in Spanish "Hoja de Cedro", the "Cedar Leaf".

The magazine is published monthly on a voluntary basis in Spanish and English, with shorter versions in Portuguese, French and Chinese, and has 1,500 subscribers internationally.

The newsletter is published under the auspices of the World Lebanese Cultural Union (WLCU) which is affiliated to the Department of Public Information of the United Nations (UN).

All copies of the Cedar Leaf, in both languages, are available for public reading in the library of the University of Notre Dame, Beirut, as well as in the library of the General Secretariat of the World Lebanese Cultural Union in Canada.

The printed version is distributed free of charge in Tranqueras Rivera (Uruguay) and Livramento (Brazil).

José María Almada Sad is a grandson of Elias Sad Saquer, who was born in 1896 in the village of Andaket, Akkar, in northern Lebanon.

Because of the oppression of the Ottoman Empire and fearing that the army would take him, Elias's mother Mariam put the 14-year old Elias on a ship to Uruguay in 1900. He was alone, without money, or knowledge of the language – as happened with so many Lebanese who immigrated to other countries.

Elias grew up working hard and later married and had a daughter Juana Adelia Sad, who married Saul Almada. His son José María was born in Tranqueras, Department (Province) Rivera, in Uruguay, on 13 November 1960.

José has worked as a journalist in Uruguay since 1978 and has trained abroad. From 2016-2018 he chaired the Lebanese Rivera Society, and has given talks and lectures on topics related to journalism and Lebanese Immigration in Uruguay and abroad.

He has received several awards for his social and volunteer work in NGOs in Uruguay and for journalism, including one from the Association of Lebanese-Mexican Intellectuals and Artists, for his worldwide work with "Hoja de Cedro".

The Lebanese South Africans salute you.

The Lebanese World salutes you.

"He who tries to dominate Lebanon will find that this tiny country is like the tiny bones of a fish. It will stick in the throat of those who are so greedy enough who want to swallow it."
Fr Paul Najm, 1979.

Franco-Lebanese Film Maker: Philippe Aractingi

Philippe Aractingi. Courtesy Wikipaedia

Philippe Aractingi is a self-taught film maker who has directed more than 50 documentaries and 4 feature films which have garnered 38 awards worldwide.

His moving response to the 2006 war in Lebanon is, "Under the Bombs", which received 23 awards including the Human Rights Film Award at the Venice Film Festival (2007).

His most recent release "Listen" (2017) is a sensual, funny, love story which explores the beauty and difficulty of a modern-day Lebanese love story.

In a world of worries, "Listen" sheds light on a form of resistance, a form of survival: love.

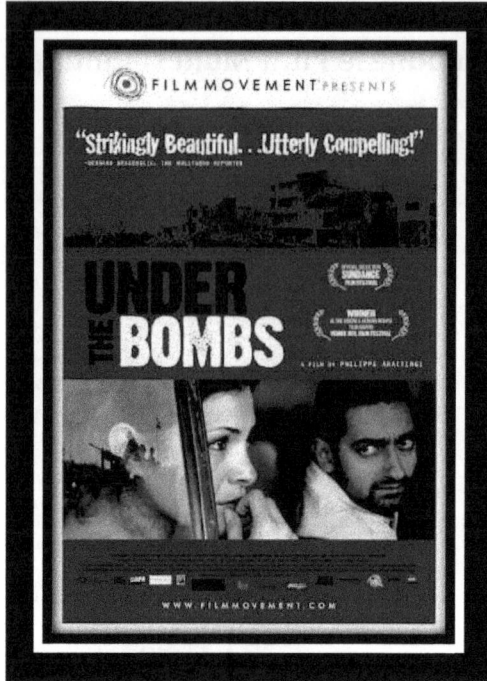

"How beautiful the brethren when they meet", said Archbishop Roland Abou Jaoude during a visit to South Africa.

On this evening the brethren were gathered for the screening of "Heritages"- a moving and powerful film by Aractingi, which explores themes of displacement, immigration, alienation, meaning of 'home' and the effects of war.

The Lebanese audience had gathered before the screening in fellowship. It was so beautiful to witness. We entered the cinema not knowing what to expect.

The Ambassador of Lebanon in South Africa His Excellency Mr. Ara Khatchadourian welcomed us all and thanked those involved in organizing the evening.

Then it happened ... the Aractingi family appeared on the stage, and Philippe spoke to Lebanese South Africans and recent arrivals from Lebanon.

It was so touching and real. One could not help but compare them – tongue in cheek – to the Von Trapp family in Austria in 1938, when they escaped from the Nazis, walked over the Alps and into freedom in Switzerland.

Now to the film. In a fresco where photos, archives and home videos subtly interact, "Heritages" depicts the sensitive topics of exile, memory and transmission, in a humorous and emotional way.

The movie which is currently being taught in schools and universities in Lebanon as a case study, is autobiographical and embraces four generations of the film maker's family, first under the Ottomans, then the French and finally the Israeli bombs.

He moves between Lebanon and France. Paramount in his mind is the family's safety and education – the same concerns experienced by previous generations.

There is much in the film to which Lebanese South Africans can relate.

Firstly, the Ottoman Empire, as their oppression was the cause of waves of Lebanese immigration. We can also relate to strong bonds of family.

And discrimination and division. Apartheid.

For the French, we can read "British" in South Africa. We also know how close we were to civil war in South Africa. We know about killing and crime.

But what we found most devastating in the film were the Israeli bombs. The devastation and the traumatizing effect they had on the morale and psychological well-being of the people.

Does Philippe have a message? Yes, that displaced persons can relate to his film.

Philippe wishes to remain in Lebanon, although his family would prefer France. A courageous decision. He looks to the Mountains of Lebanon and rises above the earth with his family, in a balloon. The balloon will remain in Lebanon.

Oh Lebanon!
How cruel that you make your home in my bones, when you know the sky and sea keep us apart.
Let me go.
But fill my lungs with the breath of my ancestors, my veins with their blood.
Keep me under your spell.

– S. Gebrael

Lebanese Wordsmiths

Arabic is a beautiful, poetic and passionate language, and Lebanon has a rich literary history. Her poets, journalists and writers - at home and abroad -are renowned for their moving, insightful, and award-winning work.

Lebanon's most famous literary 'son' is undoubtedly **Gibran Kahlil Gibran,** who hails from my village of Becharre in the Cedars of Lebanon. A philosopher, poet, writer, mystic and artist, he is best loved for his spiritual masterpiece *"The Prophet"*. His work has been translated in 40 languages and he is the third best-selling poet of all time, behind Shakespeare and Lao-Tzu.

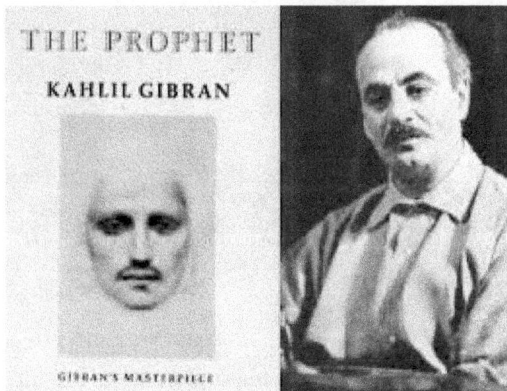

THE PROPHET
KAHLIL GIBRAN
GIBRAN'S MASTERPIECE

There are, however, many other Lebanese literary luminaries, worth reading before you die. Here are just a few gems:

Mikhail Naimy (1889-1988), a poet, novelist and philosopher, he is famous for his spiritual writings, notably *"The Book of Mirdad"*. He is widely recognized as one of the most important figures in modern Arabic letters and one of the most important spiritual writers of the 20th century.

Amin Maalouf is an award winning Lebanese-French author, whose novels focus on war and migration. *"Ports of Call"* explores the marriage of a Muslim man and Jewish woman separated in World War II.

Joumana Haddad is a journalist and women's rights activist. She was elected one of the 100 most powerful women in the Arab world by Arabian Business Magazine. Her non-fiction works: *"I Killed Scheherazade"* and *"Superman is Arab"* explore gender, feminism and the need for a renewed self-image in a changing Arab world.

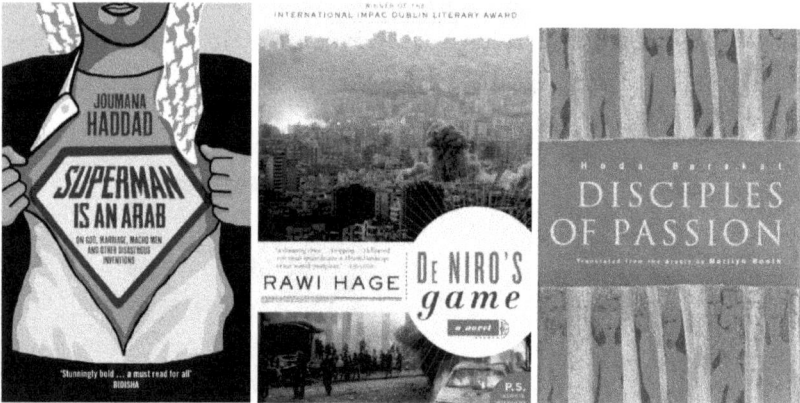

Rawi Hage is a Lebanese-Canadian photographer and author. His award-winning *"De Niro's Game"* is a dark coming of age story of two young men deciding whether to leave Beirut in the midst of Civil War.

Hoda Barakat was born in Becharre, Lebanon. Having lived in the country during the civil war, she has unique insight into the events that unfolded. *Disciples of Passion*, explores the alienation and frustration of war through the eyes of a jaded young man.

Abbas Beydoun - poet, journalist and novelist, was born near Tyre and studied at the Lebanese University and the Sorbonne, Paris. *"Blood Test"* follows the plight of a young man trying to reconnect to his roots.

Elias Khoury, playwright, critic and novelist explores politics, identity and conflict in his writing. He has lived in Lebanon, Jordan and Paris, and is one of the region's revolutionary intellectuals. *"Gates of the Sun"* tells the nostalgic story of Palestine and its conflicts.

Rabih Alammedine was born in Amman to Lebanese parents and living in Kuwait, Lebanon, England and the U.S. An engineer turned artist, he has published four books, the most famous –*"An Unnecessary Woman"*, offers fascinating insights into the life of a reclusive Lebanese woman.

Iman Humaydan is a writer, anthropologist and journalist who studied sociology in Beirut. Her novels have been translated into five languages. *"B as in Beirut"* follows the lives of four women living in the same apartment building in Beirut during the Civil war.

Emily Nasrallah was a Lebanese women's rights activist and writer of poetry, children's literature and short stories such as *"A House not her own: Stories from Beirut"*. In February 2018, shortly before her death, Nasrallah was decorated by President Michel Aoun with the Cedar Medal of Honor, Commander Rank.

CHAPTER 5

Lebanon and a Positive World Lobby

Take a Bow Lebanese South Africans

In 2015 I led a small band of Lebanese South Africans and their friends on a trip to Lebanon. Our headquarters was the "Holy Cedars of Lebanon".

The Holy part of the Holy Land. (Please remember that before 1948 there were no restrictive borders between Lebanon, Syria and present day Israel).

Here we blessed the memorial to my Jidu and Situ in the gardens in the foothills of Becharre, between Ehden and Becharre, the village that guards "The Holy Cedars" of the Lord.

My family have been in South Africa for 114 years.

At a family gathering, with the birth of a new baby, and counting my Jidu and Situ, we were seven generations of South African Lebanese. It was a time to reflect, to observe, to remember.

As a retired pharmacist, I am no longer tied to my workbench, sometimes seven days a week, so I have the opportunity to see my community at work, at play and at prayer.

What I see I like. It is tough out there, but we are in the "ball game".

Taking the four great pillars of any community, namely Family, Faith, Fellowship and Finance, I pondered how we have fared as an immigrant community.

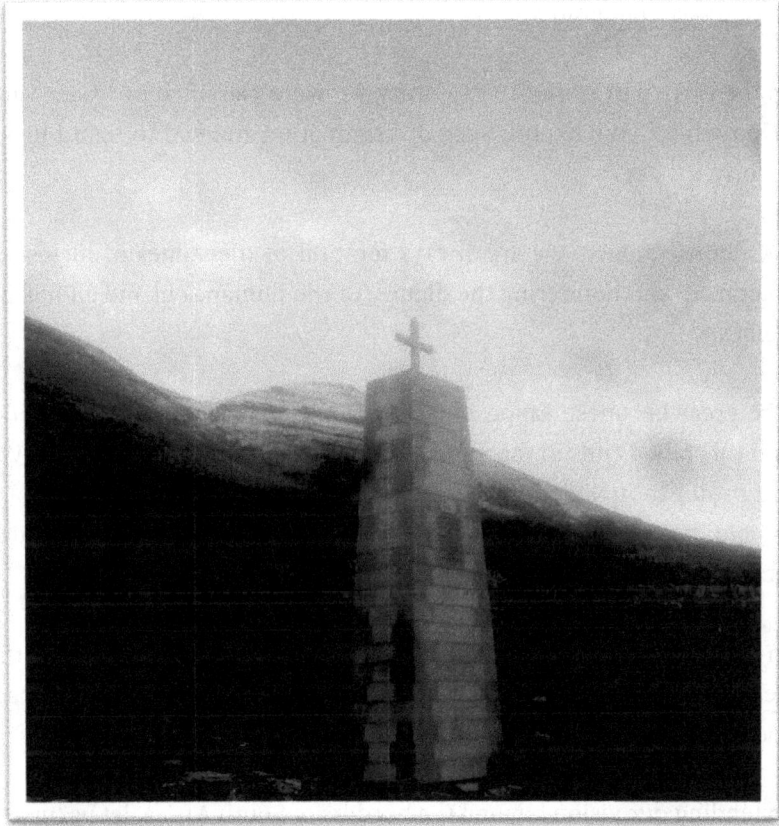

Memorial to my Jidu and Situ in The Holy Cedars of Lebanon, between Becharre and Ehden.

We have to look at our contribution, our ethos and, indeed, our vision. Yes, we have our faults and failings as Lebanese South Africans: we sold illegal liquor and have a reputation for gambling and fighting.

But, taking into account all the dynamics of a new world order, how would you rate this community? Lebanese South Africans shine brightly as immigrants.

In the early part of the 19th Century we were classified as "Asian" and "Non-white". We experienced discrimination and had to fight for our dignity.

As a consequence, we are always mindful of the values of inclusion, tolerance, and honouring the dignity of the human soul and all human beings.

The great Lebanese Empire since antiquity has been based on trade, and this blood runs in the veins of many Lebanese South Africans. We are proud to include numerous top entrepreneurs, economists, sales people, businessmen and women and a myriad of other modern day 'traders'

In my first book "People of the Cedars: A 20th Century insight into the Lebanese South Africans", I clearly demonstrate the profound impact the Lebanese have exerted on South Africa.

Extending our vision beyond the borders of South Africa, let us turn to an exciting global initiative: Lebanon and a Positive World Lobby.

There are approximately 12-16 million Lebanese worldwide. This includes 4.5 million Lebanese in Lebanon, but excludes Syrian and Palestinian refugees – raising the figure to over 6 million.

With only 10,452 km², and no possibility of ever expanding, Lebanon can never absorb 12-16 million people. We need the planet.

Please join me on a journey exploring the feasibility of a sacred world Lebanese lobby. Our starting point is Mexico City, 26 July 2014.

Professor Guita Hourani from the University of Notre Dame, Lebanon is here to promote the idea of the Lebanese as a nation and a people; Lebanon a nation dedicated to promoting dialogue between civilizations and cultures.

Guita is met by top personalities in Mexico, but her focus is on the Trabulse family and the famous quotation by Mexican President H.E. Adolpho Lopez Mateos.

Dr Guita Hourani (centre) with the Trabulse family in Mexico

The story goes that on the 21st November 1962, the Centro Lebanese in Mexico City was inaugurated with the presence of the President of Mexico who came to unveil the commemorative plaque with great enthusiasm and famously stated:

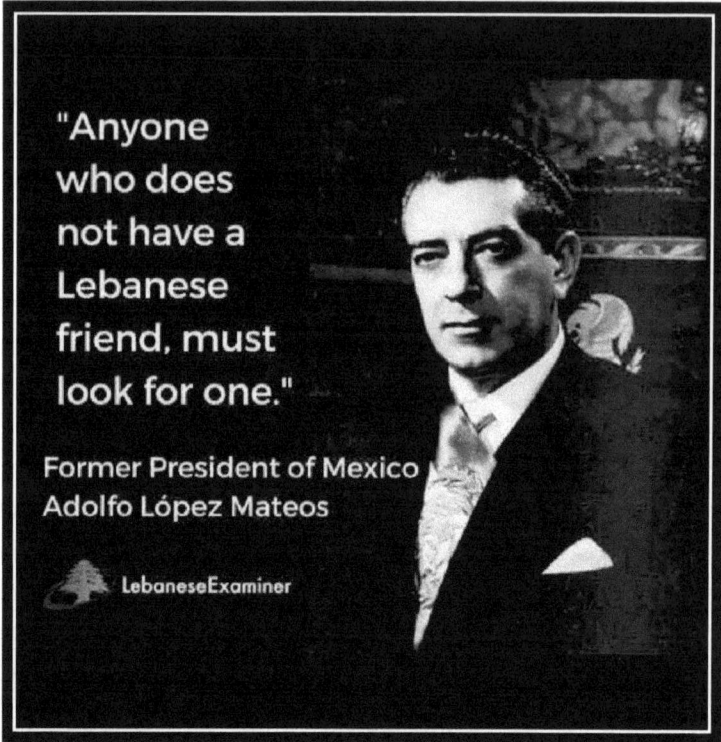

"Anyone who does not have a Lebanese friend, must look for one."

Former President of Mexico
Adolfo López Mateos

LebaneseExaminer

It seems that the sentence (above) was inspired by the relationship with many Lebanese, especially with Mr. Tufic Sayeg Attas, who was born in Zahle and is the brother-in-law of Mr. Trabulse through marrying his sister Vilma Trabulse Kaim.

Just think how many people today have a Lebanese friend?

One Lebanese Maronite Missionary Priest has over 1000 Facebook friends.

Let's be conservative: if only five million Lebanese worldwide are on Facebook, and each has 100 friends, simple arithmetic tells us that this is 500 million people.

In South Africa "People of the Cedars' wishes to add to the dialogue.

That the Lebanese become a people dedicated to promoting dialogue between civilizations, cultures, religions, and indeed a sacred world economy, which is anti-war and pro peace and fair trade.

That wishes to protect our planet for future generations.

A Sacred Economy

"We do not want a profit at all costs mentality. We need a Christian view of economic progress; respectful of human rights and which safeguards the environment"

Pope Francis, South America, 2015

We have the excellent example of our very own "Madiba" Nelson Mandela – a great friend of the Lebanese, who has given the world an example of forgiveness, love and cooperation between warring factions. He and F.W. De Klerk saved South Africa from civil war.

Pope John Paul II, when visiting Lebanon in May 1997, kissed the ground of Lebanon and stated that Lebanon is more than just a country, it is a message of hope for all humanity. Pope John Paul II, according to the Catholic Church, is now a Saint in Heaven.

Pope Francis is concerned about the growing escalation of violence in the world and is a great advocate for peace.

Many commentators say we are in the throes of a third world war.

As "People of the Cedars" we have been advised to watch our thoughts; because our thoughts become our words.

Watch our words, because our words become actions.

We must watch our emotions, because our emotions determine our character.

We must watch our character, because our character determines our destiny.

As a first step every Lebanese must think positively about Lebanon.

Please challenge anyone with any negative thoughts about Lebanon.

You know the old saying: Two men look through the same bars, one sees the mud the other the stars. Every Lebanese must see the stars.

Here in South Africa, we had the rare privilege of seeing the National Lebanese Rugby League team in action against South Africa.

South Africa is no pushover, but the Lebanese won handsomely and qualified for the Rugby League Finals in Australia and New Zealand in 2017.

But what is more important, is that South Africans saw first-hand the total cooperation and love between Muslims and Christians; native born Lebanese and Lebanese South Africans.

There were tears of joy from the elated players.

We must now ask the world to get off our backs and let us cooperate with all Lebanese.

No more divisions. Please do not try to divide and rule us.

Allow us to get on with our God given vocation.

South African Lebanese, and Lebanese South Africans have shown their commitment.

What about you?

> If Lebanon was not my country,
> I would have chosen Lebanon to
> be my country.
> *Khalil Gibran*

Lebanese Diaspora Energy in the Holy Bible

The Book of Isaiah is named after a great prophet who lived in Jerusalem in the latter half of the 8th Century BC.

He is revered in Lebanon by both Muslims and Christians. Let us turn to Chapter 23, and a message about Phoenicia (present day Lebanon).

God first destroys the great trading nation because of their pride. Lebanon is forgotten for 70 years (a terminology for a long time).

When the seventy years are over, the Lord will let Phoenicia go back to her old trade and she will hire herself out to all the kingdoms of the world.

The money she earns by commerce will be dedicated to the Lord God. She will not store it away, but those who worship the Lord will use her money to buy the food and the clothing they need.

Let us look as what the Amplified Bible has to say as a Footnote.

This whole prophesy was literally fulfilled in the following centuries. Tyre was destroyed by Nebuchadnezzar in 572 BC. The new city built on the island was taken by Alexander the Great in 332 BC. Eventually the true religion prevailed in Lebanon.

Jesus visited there (Matthew 15:21) and so did Paul (Acts 21:3-6).

Saint Jerome, writing in the fourth century AD, says that the wealth was not treasured up or hidden but was given to those who dwelt before the Lord.

Lebanese Vocation in the Modern World

Quotation: "Problems of the World can only be solved if you begin with yourselves." Cardinal Wilfred Napier, South Africa.

Let us do a little time travel together.

Four thousand years ago a Canaanite priest, Melchizedek, precursor to the modern day Lebanese, blesses the Aramaean Father of the Nation Abraham, in the name of God Most High. (Genesis 14:19)

Let us fast forward to the year 1973. Not long in the history of nations. A Lebanese President, Sleiman Franjieh, welcomes the Lebanese and the Lebanese throughout the world and refers to the two wings. That of emigration and that of the motherland. Lebanon can only rise with both wings.

Fast forward another 40 years, to 2013 and a group of visionary and concerned Lebanese businessmen and women and academics who have a vision and a dream to promote Lebanon as a nation and centre for peace-building and promoting dialogue among civilizations and cultures. The Lebanese Dialogue Initiative (LDI) is born.

The Lebanese Dialogue Initiative (LDI)

Their Mission? To call upon the United Nations (UN) to designate Lebanon as a Land of Dialogue Among Civilizations and Cultures, and to establish a universal UN center for dialogue and conflict resolution in Lebanon.

Housed at Notre Dame University-Louaize (NDU), Beirut the LDI is being implemented by the Council for Research in Values and

Philosophy; and an international academic NGO in Washington DC with major university centers in Russia, China, and Lebanon.

The LDI was officially registered as a non-governmental organization in 2015.

They are working hard to achieve their mission through mobilizing and employing the efforts of the people of Lebanon at home, as well as the goodwill of like-minded people around the world. This includes communicating with Ambassadors, Consuls, peacemakers, the Lebanese Diaspora, and International Organizations which work in the areas of peacebuilding, dialogue, reconciliation and social justice.

The Need for a Universal UN Center for Dialogue and Conflict Resolution

In April 2016, "The General Assembly and Security Council" (GASC) of the United Nations adopted ground-breaking resolutions on the role of the United Nations (UN) in peacebuilding and prevention.

These placed 'sustaining peace' at the core of UN actions and clearly stated that efforts for peace and security, sustainable development and human rights are interlinked and mutually reinforcing.

The resolutions call for the dissolution of silos and the advancement of a strongly integrated approach. The vital role of women and youth in building and sustaining peace was also emphasized.

Sustaining peace underlines the 'comprehensive, far-reaching and people-centered' vision of the transformative 2030 Agenda for Sustainable Development.

In April of 2017 the *Report of the Secretary-General on the Peacebuilding Fund,* on its commitment to providing catalytic, rapid-response, and flexible support to sustaining peace, was issued.

In addition, the UN Security Council (UNSC), one of six main organs of the UN, has as part of its mandate the following purposes: i) to maintain international peace and security; ii) develop friendly relations among nations; iii) cooperate in solving international problems and in promoting respect for human rights; and iv) be a centre for harmonizing the actions of nations.

As such, the UNSC has the prerogatives to: i) maintain international peace and security in accordance with the principles and purposes of the UN ii) investigate any dispute or situation which might lead to international friction; and iii) recommend methods of adjusting such disputes, or the terms of the settlement.

It is in the light of these United Nations resolutions that the LDI has developed its vision and mission.

Support for the Lebanese Dialogue Initiative

In his address to the United Nations in 2008, former Lebanese President H.E. Michel Sleiman stated:

> *"The philosophy of the Lebanese entity is based on dialogue, reconciliation, and coexistence."*

President Sleiman was partly inspired by a similar declaration by His Holiness St. Pope John Paul II who, on visiting Lebanon in 1995, kissed the ground and said:

> *"Lebanon is more than a country: it is a message of liberty and a paragon of pluralism for East and West alike."*

In 2006, Pope Benedict XVI stated:

"Lebanese people must rediscover their historic vocation amongst Jewish, Muslim and Christian communities."

In September 2012, during the Muslim-Christian Summit at the Maronite Patriarchate in Bkerke, religious leaders called for the designation of Lebanon as a:

"Space for dialogue among civilizations based on peace and diversity."

The distinguished Muslim scholar, Ayatollah Sheikh Mohammad Mehdi Shamseddine, once said:

"There is no Lebanon without its Christians, and no Lebanon without its Muslims"

In 2017 Lebanese Prime Minister Saad Hariri called Lebanon "a model of coexistence."

In 2013, Hon. Consul Zard Abou Jaoude contributed towards the establishment of an organization which embodies and instils the idea of designating Lebanon as a Land of Dialogue Among Civilizations and Cultures – an initiative originally conceived by Consul Abou Jaoude and H.E. the late Ambassador Fouad Turk.

In 2017 President, H.E. Gen. Michel Aoun, expressed his support for the LDI. In his state address to the United Nations General Assembly, he stated that a center for dialogue and conflict resolution in Lebanon would "serve humanity". He re-iterated this support again in his official meeting with Pope Francis in the Vatican in the same year.

Secretary-General of the UN, H. E. António Guterres, in turn expressed the support of the United Nations for such a request.

Throughout its campaign across more than 60 countries since 2013, the LDI has garnered support from prominent figures such as Lebanese Patriarch Bechara Boutros Rahi, Secretary General of the Arab League Ahmed Aboul Gheit; Australian Governor-General Peter Cosgrove; and the Delegation of the European Union to Beirut.

These declarations and many others have resonated among Lebanon's various ethnic and religious communities, a vast majority of whom have adopted these as the ultimate vocation of Lebanon and its people.

Lebanon, in fact, has paradoxically become somewhat of a universal symbol for both fruitful intercultural global dialogue and for the complete breakdown of all civility.

Such calls are not simply idealizations of Lebanon's past or present vocation, but are rooted in facts reaching far back into its history.

In the last century and a half, Lebanon has experienced various socio-political systems that were born out of the womb of suffering and the will to find peaceful solutions to protect freedom of religion and diversity.

With the Pact of 1943 it was decided that the President of the Republic of Lebanon would be a Maronite Christian, the Prime minister a Sunni Muslim, and the Speaker of the House of Parliament a Shiite Muslim.

While this 'Confessional" political system is not without its challenges and critics, it remains a unique attempt at inclusion.

Lebanon's population is composed of eighteen ethno-religious groups (Jews, Christians, Muslims, Druze and others) and in the last thirty years Lebanon has recognized new groups under the law to acknowledge their freedom of religion. Labour migration has added to Lebanon's religious and ethnic diversity (Hindus, Buddhists, and Sikhs) that freely practice their faith.

This diversity is Lebanon's great strength and weakness, as its painful modern history attests, and is precisely what makes it worthy of being designated a land of dialogue among civilizations and cultures.

In general, Lebanese do not perceive diversity as a threat but rather as an opportunity to be enriched, hence their predisposition to continue and to spearhead this dialogue (with a particular focus on Muslim-Christian dialogue) in the Middle East.

Depiction of Al-Hakim, founder of the Druze, a mysterious, 1,000 year old religion with approx. 270,000 followers in Lebanon

The Lebanese people and their struggle to live freely has often been an inspiration and a liberating force for others in the region. Their communities all over the world have been recognized as exemplary by their host countries in terms of promoting dialogue and openness to diversity.

Lebanon's raison d'etre is founded on the paradigm of understanding, freedom and conviviality among civilizations and cultures. In spite of the challenges to its vocation, which at times have resulted in tragic failures, the world has much to learn from Lebanon's historical experiences.[6]

Objectives and Current Efforts

- LDI is encouraging the Government of Lebanon to send an official request to the UN Secretary-General for the UN to establish a universal center for dialogue and conflict resolution in Lebanon.
- To encourage dialogue in the spirit of the UN Universal Declaration of Human Rights among civilizations and cultures as a contribution to peaceful coexistence among groups.
- To raise public awareness of the spirit and culture of dialogue through social and print media.
- To promote the LDI among the Lebanese Diaspora and to benefit from its strong presence and visibility.
- To promote the LDI among like-minded people and organizations around the world.
- To create a platform to facilitate international collaborative seminars and research workshops.
- To examine a wide range of religious, ethnic, racial and cultural dialogue activities and to disseminate the outcome through publications.
- To initiate research projects and conduct seminars/courses that focus on the spirit and culture of the Initiative, in

---

[6] Adapted from information provided by the LDI initiative. With grateful thanks to Dr Guita Hourani.

cooperation with academic institutions and international organizations, e.g. that held at NDU on Relational Needs, emphasizing the philosophical and psychological meaning of dialogue (2013/14).

- To support local, regional and international conferences related to the Initiative. These have included "Interreligious/ Intercultural Dialogue: Reflections on the Nature of Love and Forgiveness". NDC (2013), and "The Dialogue of Civilizations with an Emphasis on Lebanon", and "The Legacy of Chinua Achebe: Dialogical Explorations in Philosophy, Literature, and Politics", attended by Nobel Prize Winner in Literature, Wole Soyinka. 2014, Sao Paulo, Brazil.

- LDI has been successful in its diplomacy efforts. Since 2016, the "Dialogue and Best Practice International Forum (2016 and 2017)" has hosted diplomats and senior negotiators from Kosovo, Serbia, and Northern Ireland in dialogue tables to discuss their experiences with conflict and dialogue, as well as garner their support of the initiative.

- LDI is planning its third annual forum for November 2018 and continuing with its programs and activities.

> *"Out of suffering have emerged the strongest souls; the most massive characters are seared with scars."*
>
> *Kahlil Gibran*

Break Down the Walls by Ken Hanna

The Don wants a wall in the USA
to keep Mexican Workers away.

Benjie built a wall in Palestine –
The Don says: 'OK, everything's fine'.

The Don says Jerusalem must be
only for Zionists, not free.

129 countries of the world in unison say,
The Don simply cannot act that way.

And what about all the Christian folk
and that Jerusalem may go up in smoke?
And occupied Palestine does exist:
12 million people are real and resist.

Poems a plenty our people write,
to encourage folk in their rightful fight.

Come what may, we'll remain in the fray.
A 'One State Solution' is now a must,
for Jews and Muslims and Christians it's just.

Listen to Lebanon so dear,
Her wisdom and truth are so clear.
Where Christians, Muslims and Druze
Conflict, fighting and strife they refuse.

Take a leaf out of South Africa's choice:
Let Palestine talk with one voice.
From the ANC they can learn,

when it comes to their inevitable turn.

Abandon the arms race please,
then the world can live in peace.
Jerusalem a capital for all,
So all in the world can walk tall.

Thank God for a Jesus so pure,
He loves all mankind for sure.
With the Holy Quran let us agree,
because it sets all Muslims free.
Islam means 'Peace' you know,
Which on their followers they wish to bestow.

Let everyone have a small home,
So refugees don't have to roam.

Lebanon has the answer you know:
She says to her daughters and sons:
Come drink from the fountains
and walk in the mountains.

Dialogue between cultures and civilizations
is what builds great and strong Nations.

Lebanon the heart that pumps the blood of life
to a world so full of pain and strife.
It is food we need and refugees we'll feed.
It is clothes on your back, so you'll need no rucksack.

With Gibran and Mandela,
Lebanon and SA are two great solutions.
But it will need a bold person to say:
"We need resolutions and a World Revolution"

Lebanese Women and a Positive World Lobby

Magazine Queen: Patricia Bitar Cherfan

"The beauty of our country is that Lebanon is big enough to fill the whole world, and yet small enough to remain at a human scale, where anyone of us can make a difference, an impact."

These are the words of dynamic magazine founder and editor, Patricia Bitar Cherfan, whose fantastic magazine "Home" specializes in promoting Lebanon and Lebanese talents of the world, and reaching out to connect Lebanese around the globe. The magazine covers all aspects of life in Lebanon, from style, to culture, to heritage, to business, to people, and especially the "giving back side of life". Patricia is also Chairman and Managing Director of PiDRAYA, a visionary social enterprise promoting sustainable development. PiDRAYA was the Phoenician Goddess of light, and it is light that Patricia spreads with her passion, vivacity, vision and energy.

Lebanon's African Diamond Lady: Caroline Sasseen

This story begins in Tripoli, Lebanon in 1857, when Khalil Ibrahim Sasseen is born. At a tender age he marries Wahibe Badwe Nasser, and as he is a general dealer by trade, he travels to several countries.

In 1892 in Tasmania, an Australian Island and state, at the age of 35 he receives his Certificate of Naturalisation for the purpose of trading. The same year he travels to South Africa and in 1908, after 16 years of residence, he receives his South African Certificate of Naturalisation which permits and admits an alien to the position and rights of citizenship and invests them with the privileges of a native born subject.

This is the beginning of many great advantages for Khallil. During these years he travels back and forth to Lebanon, where his four children Toufic, Najieb, Mary and Egine are born.

Toufic Khallil Sasseen follows in his father's footsteps and is already trading in South Africa in 1905. In 1924 he marries Mary Adami of Jounieh, Lebanon and the couple has 5 sons: Khallil, Joseph, Thomas (Tommy), Michael and George.

Khallil Toufic Sasseen enters the field of diamonds and jewellery, and later known as 'Callie', marries Dawn Rosella and together they have four children.

Our focus is on Caroline and her entry into the diamond and jewellery business and her service to the Lebanese South African Community.

Caroline has been described as dynamic, unique, intelligent, available, dependable, very well informed, helpful and very sincere.

She is on top of her game. She networks and sparkles. She is conversant with Arabic and fluent in English. As one commentator said: 'Not only does she sell diamonds, she is the purest diamond of them all'.

But it is for service to the Lebanese and Arabic world that Caroline is well known: she is the Leader of the Lebanese Community in Kwa-Zulu Natal and backbone of the Lebanese Maronite Mission in the province.

Caroline – with her two sisters, Michelle and Linda – organizes regular Holy Mass and delightful social gatherings of Lebanese from all over South Africa who congregate at the holiday hub of Umhlanga Rocks.

"People of the Cedars" salutes Lebanon's African Diamond and Gold Princess.

Marathon Runner and Peace Activist: May El-Khalil

Another visionary Lebanese woman is May El-Khalil: Lebanon's Marathon queen. Now settled in Lebanon, May is a Lebanese Nigerian. She too wishes to contribute positively to Lebanon and its World image. Her philosophy: Lots of water, greens, laughter, optimism, love and sports. She adds a new dimension to Lebanese femininity and a dynamic that is awe-inspiring.

In 2003 May El-Khalil, a local sports official, decided it was time to start a marathon open to all, as an antidote to sectarianism.

And despite ongoing political and security pressure, the Beirut Marathon, now entering its 15th year, has become not only the largest running event in the Middle East, but a powerful force for peace.

May was inspired to start the marathon after a personal tragedy: a near-fatal running accident. Doctors told her she would never run again.

She was hospitalized for two years and had to undergo a long series of surgeries. But her resolve from this personal struggle created an event that, each year, draws runners and fans from opposing political and religious communities in a symbolic act of peace.

Case in point: In 2012, on a rainy and windy November day, more than 33,000 runners turned out. Other countries around the region are now thinking of replicating this model.

"Indeed, as the Middle East fractures under the weight of disparity, the Beirut Marathon continues to unite." — Debra Witt, Runner's World

Lebanon's Lady Genius – Dialogue, Dream, Vision:

Dr Guita G. Hourani

Another inspiring, dedicated and visionary Lebanese woman is Dr Guita G. Hourani.

Dr Hourani is Secretary-General and Director of the International Campaign: Lebanon Land of Dialogue among Civilizations and Cultures.

Dr Hourani is a world expert on Lebanese migration, and on migration from, to and through Lebanon, and is founder and Director of the Lebanese Emigration Research Center (LERC). With extensive resources and archives LERC is a prominent center on Lebanese migration in the world. In 2005 the Lebanon and Migration Museum was opened, followed by the Lebanese Migration Gallery of Art in 2010.

Dr Hourani is also a leading scholar in the area of Maronite Christian history, founding in 1995 the first research centre on the Maronites, and publishing the first English electronic (open access) journal on the Maronites "The Journal of Maronite Studies" in 1997.

Dr Hourani holds a PhD from the Graduate School of Global Studies, Tokyo University of Foreign Studies, Japan.

She is also assistant Professor at the Faculty of Law and Political Science at Notre Dame University, Lebanon.

Dr Guita Hourani

While in the USA as an International Development Consultant at the World Bank she pioneered a course on the role of women in war, peace and conflict resolution, which she taught at various universities and institutions.

Her current research projects include: State Sovereignty, Security and Refugees in the case of Lebanon; Survival of the Kurds in Lebanon Pre and Post Naturalization; and Lebanese return-migration and adaptation post Taif.

Dr Hourani has conducted research, and given lectures and papers, in more than 24 countries on projects related to migration, refugees, socio-economic mobility, political participation, human insecurity, integration policies and access to information, among others.

Dr Hourani has served fellowships at leading universities internationally and has received numerous awards and commendations for her work.

What makes me myself rather than anyone else is the very fact that I am poised between two countries, two or three languages, and several cultural traditions.
It is precisely this that defines my identity.
Would I exist more authentically if I cut off a part of myself.

Amin Maalouf, Lebanese Author

For if our past be forgotten

And our heritage destroyed,

Will not our future be moulded by our enemies?

From: "Listen to the Arab Cry"

Islam and the Glorious Quran

"Strongest among men in enmity to the believers wilt thou find the Jews and Pagans; and nearest among them in love to the believers wilt thou find those who say, 'We are Christians': because amongst these are men devoted to learning and men who have renounced the world, and they are not arrogant".

Quran, Chapter 5 verse 82, translation Yusuf Ali.

The Quran is referring to the Noble Christians of Lebanon.

Muhammad, founder of Islam, was born in AD 570 and died in AD 632.

He was born in Mecca in Arabia. His father died before he was born, and he was cared for by his grandfather Abdullah ibn Abdul-Muttalib and after his grandfather's death by his uncle, Abu Talib.

As a young boy he travelled to Syria and Lebanon then known as Al Sham al Kabir - in his uncle's merchant caravan. Later he made the same journey in the service of a wealthy widow named Khadijah, whom he later married.

Historical sources describe how Muhammad met a Monophysite monk in Syria – Rahib Bahira – who had an influence on his prayer life.

Bahira also foretold to the adolescent Muhammad his future as a prophet based on his observation of the movement of a cloud that kept shadowing Muhammad regardless of the time of day.

It became Muhammad's practice to retire during the hot month every year with his family to a cave in the desert for meditation.

His place of retreat was Hira, a desert hill not far from Mecca, and his chosen month was Ramadan, the month of heat.

There was a large Jewish community in Arabia at that time. The Arabian people worshiped idols.

It was in Hira, towards the end of his quiet month at the age of 40 that the Archangel Gabriel, God's messenger, appeared to Muhammad. It was the first revelation.

Over a period of 22 years the Archangel Gabriel communicated the Glorious Quran.

The Archangel appeared to Muhammad for two reasons: to bring the concept of the worship of the One God and to obey His message, and to encourage the Jewish people of Arabia to become inclusive and not exclusive.

According to Father Christopher Clohessy, a South African and Professor at the Pontifical Institute for Arabic and Islamic Studies in Rome, the most respectful way for a Christian to speak or write of Muhammad is: "Muhammad, the Prophet of Islam, peace be upon Him". The phrase: "Peace be upon Him" can be written (PBUH).

Father Christopher further writes that the Holy Quran remains, primarily, what it always has been for millions of Muslims, The Book of God.

It is the text held sacred by millions that lies at the very heart of Islam. It is the text that Islam regards as God's own speech made audible and visible. For Muslims, the Quran is both the source of truth and guide for embodying truth in the actions of one's daily life.

Muslims draw the language of their faith, their devotional and spiritual life, and the practical application for living justly, wisely and with balance in a complex world, deeply engaged with justice and equality, from the Quran.

It offers for Muslims the essential structure of daily life, reminding faithful Muslims each day that God has spoken to people and people have heard God's voice.

"Our Christian response to the Quran, and to the faith that it constructs in countless lives, should always be one of reverence and respect", says Father Christopher. "The Church regards with esteem also the Muslim (one who submits to God)".

In the document 'Nostra Aetate' of Vatican Council II, Blessed Paul VI in his 'Ecclesiam Suam' writes of Muslims being "deserving of our admiration for all that is true and good in the worship of God".

Saint John Paul II refers more than once to the Quran as "the sacred book" or as "Holy".

Roadmap for Dialogue with Islam

Islam means 'Peace'

Referring to Islam, Bishop Miguel Ayuso Guixot, secretary of the Pontifical Council for Interreligious dialogue, says:

> *"Its landmarks are peace, justice, education and identity, which should always be preserved and valued".*

We note that Jesus is mentioned 25 times in the Quran and our Blessed Lady, the Mother of Jesus 70 times.
Called Maryam by Muslims, Mary is the only woman to be referred to by her first name.

For example, our Blessed Mother is described as born without original sin.

> *"And Mary, the daughter of 'Imran, who guarded her chastity... she believed in the words of her Lord and His scriptures and was of the devoutly obedient. Quran 66:12*

We love the Arabic language. It is our language; the language that Christian and Muslim Lebanese brothers and sisters share.

The five pillars of Islam: Shahadah (profession of faith), Salah (prayer), Zakat (support of the poor and needy), Sawm (fasting), Hajj (pilgrimage to Mecca) and seeking knowledge as a religious duty, are respected by all Lebanese.

Receiving your friends with a smile is a form of charity, says the Prophet in the Hadith (various collected accounts of the sayings, actions and habits of the Prophet Muhammad).

It is estimated that by 2050 there will be equal numbers of Muslims and Christians globally – the vast majority of believers in the world.

During May of 2016, in a one-on-one interview with "People of the Cedars" in South Africa, H.E. Cardinal and Patriarch His Eminence Becharra Boutros el Rahi, Father of Antioch and all the East stated that Lebanon has agreed on a 50/50 partnership of Christians and Muslims.

Muhammad (PBUH) remains a mighty Arabian leader. One of the great figures of history is so poorly appreciated in the Christian West.
Ssadly the faith and its followers are often subjected to misinformation for political and monetary interests. It is called Islamaphobia,

Islam and the vast majority of devout Muslims are full of humanity, piety and modesty.

Pope Francis (right) with the Grand Imam Ahmed Tayyib
taken at Vatican City Nov. 2017

*"I love you when you bow
in your mosque, kneel in
your temple, pray in your
church. For you and I are
sons of one religion, and it
is the Spirit."*

Kahlil Gibran,

"The Prophet"

Two Wings: By Ken Hanna

Muslims and Christians are Lebanon's eyes.
They will not fight if they are wise.
Those who try to tear them apart
Have black and envious hearts.

"Divide and rule" our enemies say –
This is always corruption's way.

Christians and Muslims are Lebanon's ears
To hear the wisdom of God they revere.
Muslims pray five times a day,
This they believe is one of God's ways.

And nod to Christians who exclaim:
It has to be love which comes from
The Almighty above.

In Lebanon Jesus turned water to wine,
Transfigured from human into Divine.
Muhammad for Muslims reigns most high,
Their lifestyle devout, humble, refined.

Both Christians and Muslims respect
Blessed Mary so pure, who
Nurtures and protects them, for sure.

Muslims and Christians are Lebanon's wings,
In their flight they learn to forgive,
And rise in faith above strife and sin.

Christians and Muslims – the country's pride,
On their true hearts Lebanon's future rides.

"I should like now to greet the young Muslims who are with us this evening. I thank you for your presence, which is so important. Together with the young Christians, you are the future of this fine country and of the Middle East in general. Seek to build it up together! And when you are older, continue to live in unity and harmony with Christians. For the beauty of Lebanon is found in this fine symbiosis. It is vital that the Middle East in general, looking at you, should understand that Muslims and Christians, Islam and Christianity, can live side by side without hatred, with respect for the beliefs of each person, so as to build together a free and humane society"

Pope Benedict XVI, September 15, 2012, in the Square across from the Maronite Patriarchate of Bkerké in an address to a large crowd of Lebanese young people.

Moses and Madiba: Liberators of Africa

Africa is, today, one of the great areas of growth of the Christian faith, with approximately 599 million Christians (2018), more than either Latin America or Europe.

It is so important for Africans to realize that Moses, one of the key Biblical figures in the "Economy of Salvation" – the plan of salvation as directed by God Most High – was an African.

In the Synchronous History of the Bible, Catholic Edition, it is noted that Moses was born in Egypt in 1300 BC. In 1750 BC Jacob and 70 descendants entered Egypt (Genesis 46:27). God, in his wisdom, had changed Jacob's name to Israel, "for you have striven with God and with humans and have prevailed". So Moses was an Israelite African.

In the space of only 450 years the Israelites multiplied to over 600,000 men, besides women and children, becoming a fully-fledged nation (Exodus12:37). As South Africans we can understand a time span of 450 years – the length of time since the first white settlers came to this country – and can also see how we have developed during this time.

Moses was an African believer in the concept of one God, and the one to whom the Almighty God gave the Ten Commandments at Mount Sinai. Interestingly Moses's wife, Zipporah, was a Midianite (Arabian), and her father Jethro was a High Priest of Midian (Exodus18:1).

The Egyptians, however, considered their Pharaohs (Kings) to be their 'Gods'. So we see that the journey of the Israelites was not only *from* political slavery in Egypt, but also *to* religious freedom of belief.

Once again, Lebanese South Africans can relate to this as we came to this country fleeing from religious oppression, conflict and persecution in Lebanon.

While Moses was an Israelite African, Nelson Mandela (affectionately known by all South Africans as 'Madiba') was a Methodist South African. He received the "Baptism of the Spirit" whilst in jail on Robben Island. According to Pastor Ray McCauley, a leading Evangelist and friend of Madiba's, it could be why South Africa was saved from civil war.

Just as Moses freed the Israelites from slavery and from religious oppression in Egypt, so Mandela freed black South Africans from the ideological and political 'slavery' of Apartheid.

Moses never entered the Promised Land of Canaan (the area comprising Palestine and present day Lebanon and Syria).

Mandela, however, lived to see the liberation of his beloved people and country with the birth of democracy in 1994.

Moses is respected by Christians, Muslims and Jews. Mandela, too, is loved and respected by all religious persuasions in South Africa and the world.

Jesus and the Rocky Heights of Lebanon

In Memoriam: Nelson Rolihlahla Mandela

18 July 1918 – 5 December 2013

It was December 2013. And we were mourning and celebrating the life and times of Nelson Mandela.

Lebanese South Africans, all South Africans and indeed the world gave grateful thanks to God for giving us this great leader.

We thanked Madiba for saving South Africa.

As I stood in the Hall of Remembrance of our beloved Madiba in Johannesburg in silence and contemplation, I prayed that I may dedicate my life to what he stood for: love, compassion, reconciliation and inclusivity, not exclusivity.

But Madiba also believed, when those in power would not listen, in the armed struggle. And so Madiba spent 27 years in prison on Robben Island, off the shore of Cape Town.

Mandela emerged as a saint of our age; a holy person, a very good, patient and unselfish person.

He also emerged as a very strong, determined and committed person. The greats of the world are humbled by his strength of character.

Of royal blood, Madiba went to a Catholic School and was a devout Christian in the Methodist persuasion.

On Robben Island he led a monastic spiritual life under harsh and inhumane conditions. He toiled in those painful lime quarries.

There is a painting in Houghton Johannesburg depicting Martin Luther King, Abraham Lincoln, Churchill, Obama, Mandela, John F Kennedy, and Gandhi. Mandela outshines them all.

As I made my way to Madiba's home in 12th street, the flowers were withering and the crowds diminishing.

Please. We the "People of the Cedars" of South Africa must never fade or diminish.

We the Lebanese people in South Africa have our beloved Madiba.

We have Gibran Kahlil Gibran.

We have Saint Charbel – and we have the rocky heights of Lebanon.

We have the one we call Lord and Master: Jesus the Christ.

As we mentally stand on those rocky heights of Lebanon, we look to the South, we look to the North, we look to the East and we look to the West.

We humbly add our contribution to the community of nations in our quest for world peace.

Garden of Eden in Lebanon

According to Terje Stordalen
(University of Oslo),
Eden in Ezekiel appears to be
located in Lebanon.
Possibly Ehden, near
Becharre in the "Cedars of
Lebanon".

CHAPTER 6

Lebanese Diaspora Energy (LDE) Initiative

A Global movement strengthening Socio-Cultural and Economic bonds among the Lebanese

The LDE is an initiative launched by the Lebanese Ministry of Foreign Affairs and Emigrants in 2014 during the tenure of Minister Gebran Bassil.

It was established to strengthen the cultural, social and economic bonds between Lebanese in the Homeland and emigrants in the Diaspora internationally, to showcase the success stories of Lebanese residents and expatriates, celebrate the Lebanese heritage and promote a positive image of Lebanon around the world.

During LDE conferences around the globe, Lebanese key players and decision-makers from the Diaspora connect and share investment opportunities in Lebanon and abroad.

This opportunity to network with peers in similar sectors worldwide, also allows for establishing lobbying initiatives and participating in foreign policy-making regarding the Diaspora.

When launching the initiative, Minister Bassil called on the Lebanese Diaspora to preserve Lebanese culture and language, to support the creation of the Museum of the Emigrants in the homeland and Lebanese Diaspora schools around the world; to contribute to the Lebanese Diaspora Fund and "work with us to invest in Lebanon" and to use the Lebanon Connect platform to "promote social and economic exchange with Lebanese all around the world".

He also stressed the importance of preserving Lebanese land: "When we lose our land we lose our anchor. The land is what keeps us together," he said.

Lebanese Emigration Research Centre (LERC)

The Lebanese Emigration Research Centre is an academic initiative of Notre Dame University (NDU) established in April 2003.

It is dedicated to the study of migration.

The creation of the centre is a direct result of the NDU's awareness of the Lebanese emigrant's contribution to their ancestral land and to their new home countries.

It is also the result of NDU's awareness of a renewed interest in global identity, ancestral roots, and genealogical heritage.

> *"Love is the law of God. You live that you may learn to love. You love that you may learn to live. No other lesson is required of Man."*
>
> From *"The Book of Mirdad"*, Mikhail Naimy (1889- 1988), Lebanese author famous for his spiritual writings.

Gebran Bassil, Lebanese Minister of Foreign Affairs
Statesman and Darling of the Lebanese World

Gebran Bassil was born on 21st June 1970 in Batroun, Lebanon. He is a Christian Maronite who holds a Master's Degree in Civil Engineering from the American University of Beirut. He is married to Chantale Michel Aoun, daughter of the current President of Lebanon H.E. General Michel Aoun (elected November 2017). They have three children. He is Lebanon's Minister of Foreign Affairs and leader of Lebanon's Free Patriotic Movement.

Our Lebanity exceeds borders. It is not a geographic entity. It is a human entity that has the world as its borders. It is a love of a nation. It is a passion for public work. It is an oasis of HOME. **Gebran Bassil, 2016**

Lebanese Diaspora Energy Conference, Johannesburg Feb. 2017

2017 was an historic year for Lebanon and the Lebanese Diaspora, as well as for me personally.

The first Lebanese Diaspora Energy Conference in Africa was held in February 2017 in Johannesburg South Africa, just a short distance from my place of residence.

Over 400 delegates converged on our Lebanese Community in South Africa from all parts of Africa.

It was a stimulating and awe-inspiring experience to witness great Lebanese minds invest their energy, expertise, knowhow and their 'Lebanity' in the African pond.

The Lebanese ambassador to South Africa – H.E. Ara Khatchadourian and his wife Myriam – were at their very best organizing functions and dinners. The Lebanese in South Africa, it was clear, were batting in a very high league.

And one was always mindful of the presence of Gebran, who was fast becoming the darling of the Lebanese World, and a great statesman.

He was to visit the Southern tip of the African Continent, in Cape Town, where my Jidu and Situ from Becharre had arrived from Lebanon some 114 years previously to make their home in South Africa.

What was so significant is that the Lebanese in Cape Town stood on the tables and declared their Lebanity – their Lebanese identity and heritage – amidst great applause.

An identity in the minds and the hearts of true Lebanese. No money on earth can buy this. It is a gift from the Almighty God.

"Lebanese people are marked by a real odyssey; full of travels and adventures, which makes their stories wider than their territory."

Roberto Khatlab; author of the first complete guide to Lebanon in the Portuguese language "Lebanon: An Oasis in the Middle East. A touristic, historical, archaeological, cultural and religious guide".

Lebanese Indaba, Beirut, May 2017

Just three months later, we made our way to Lebanon for the Beirut Lebanese Indaba, where some 3,500 delegates from over 100 countries descended on Lebanon.

Over 100 of the top intellectuals and brains in the world attended and presented outstanding papers embracing relevant world topics of interest and inter-Lebanese dialogue.

To be with my fellow Lebanese South Africans, to meet with The President of the Republic of Lebanon H.E. Michel Aoun, with Lebanon's Prime Minister H.E. Saad Hariri and other Lebanese Leaders, was a great honour.

We travelled to Batroun in North Lebanon to The Lebanese Diaspora village where guests from around the world enjoyed a magnificent Lebanese luncheon.

We were again in the presence of our beloved Gebran, and whilst we were shown how to grow Cedar Trees, I heard a Lebanese school teacher from Australia say that we were witnessing the future president of Lebanon in action.

Lebanese Diaspora Village

This historic initiative in Batroun – a scenic coastal city in North Lebanon – is the creative brainchild of Minister Bassil and the Municipality of Batroun.

The vision is for countries in the Diaspora with large Lebanese communities to 'adopt' one of nine beautiful old houses in the village and renovate and furnish them in the style of their adopted home country.

The communities who have engaged with the project have provided financial support to ensure the success of the project, and in turn have a place to celebrate and honour the achievements of the Lebanese in the Diaspora. Private donors have also supported the project, such as my beloved cousin the late Roy Hanna of Johannesburg.

The village is a venue for exhibitions, trade shows, festivals and events, and boasts a museum, a small hotel, a café, and a place where communities in the Diaspora can come together to exchange ideas and collaborate. In May 2017 Gebran Bassil inaugurated houses for the USA, United Arab Emirates, Canada, Brazil, West Africa and, of course, South Africa.

The Diaspora Museum

The centrepiece of the project is the Lebanese Diaspora Museum, which contains artefacts from the history of Lebanese emigration. Lebanese in the Diaspora are encouraged to donate artefacts from family history to the museum, contributing to an understanding and appreciation of the emigrant experience.

According to Dr Guita Hourani, director of the Lebanese Emigration Research Center (LERC), more important than the population numbers in the Diaspora, are the accomplishments, contributions and visibility of the Lebanese.

"This is where the phenomenon is – a small population of emigrants who succeeded in every immigration country," said Hourani. "A village dedicated to their success has much to celebrate".

Gebran Bassil, Lebanese Foreign Minister (right) with the
author, Cape Town, 2017

Lebanese Sayings:

"The pot has found its cover", meaning two people
connect well.

"There's bread and salt between us", meaning two
people are close to each other.

Lebanese: A Noble Responsibility

Editorial by Ali H. Shami Seattle, Washington.
As appeared in 'Cedar Leaf', Lebanese immigrants and their
descendants; Rivera; Tranqueras, Uruguay, edited by José María
Almada Sad.

When I started writing this editorial about my experience as a
Lebanese emigrant, I froze for a few minutes and did not know what to
write. Getting asked by the World Lebanese Cultural Union (WLCU)
to write the editorial by itself is a great honour. Writing something of
worth to match only a sliver of the achievements of the WLCU is an
even greater task. As I embarked into this journey, I said to myself that
this is probably going to be one of the most challenging tasks;
especially with the ongoing turmoil in Lebanon. All of a sudden, a
series of positive memories started rolling in front of my eyes and
washed away the negative thoughts. The chain of events and past
experiences led me to 1st January 1985 when I arrived at the
University of Alabama coming from Lebanon carrying one piece of
luggage, my Lebanese passport, and a hole in my heart which I had left
back home. I did not know that the next few hours would present a
positive experience that would be engraved in my mind until the day
I die. The feelings associated with that experience occurred one more
time in my life when I attended my first WLCU conference in Victoria,
Canada several years ago. An experience that made me so proud of not
only being a Lebanese but also lucky to have experienced an example
of how the Lebanese emigrants are such a great source of hope to
those living in Lebanon and abroad! Walking down the University
strip with rain drops falling on my shoulders, I could see a glimpse of
the International House where I was supposed to report. Having
struggled for months in Beirut before I made it out of the ailing
country Lebanon to come to the United States with few hundred
dollars in my pocket, nothing was going to stop me from pursuing my
dreams as a Lebanese American. I walked into the International

House and introduced myself to Mr. Greg: the admission officer. As soon as I said that I came from Lebanon, he reached for his desk phone, called someone, and said: "Hi, one of your fellow Lebanese young men is here". Within 15 minutes, I saw a Chevrolet stopping in front of the International House. A young man got out of the car and hollered:"Alloush! Ahla wsahla!" This young man swiftly reached for my luggage, picked it up and put it in his car. Standing there and hearing the Lebanese accent that I had not heard for the last two days while travelling through strange lands was such a great relief! He assured me that I was in good hands with a wonderful group of Lebanese people. Every time I expressed my sincere appreciation he would say 'no worries' and that there was no need to even mention his name. He said he was only paying back by paying forward! For this reason, I will continue to refer to him as the Lebanese 'young man'. We arrived to his apartment to find over ten Lebanese waiting for us. I will never forget that diverse group of Lebanese new friends: Sunnis, Shia, Christian, Druze all sitting together. For the whole three weeks following my arrival, they fought not only over who would be my host, but also helped me to obtain my first driver's license, made me familiar with the campus, and explained the university academic rules in detail. I sat there being mesmerized by how well they treated me and talked with each other! As soon as I settled down and moved to my own apartment, I joined them in welcoming the new students coming from Lebanon. I wanted the new students to feel the same way I did. I wanted them to know how Lebanon back home can and should be! Why did I have the urge to share this personal story? In my perspective, Lebanon is great not because of its history and climate but because of its genuine and nice people.

> "Lebanon is great because at every single moment there is a Lebanese somewhere around the world making a difference and impacting someone else's life".

From that day, I decided to look for the positive Lebanese people who love Lebanon and decided to connect with those who love humanity even more. Lebanon's history is a high bar that we should always strive to reach. It is a great history that deserves a great present and a greater future. It is not only a privilege to be a Lebanese but it is also a noble responsibility. Nothing is more uplifting to my spirit than seeing successful Lebanese women and men soaring with their heads up high but also grounded with humility and guided by their love for their fellow human beings. For Lebanon where I took my first breath as an infant, I say 'I will never forget you'. For the United States of America, which I consider home I say 'I am proud and grateful'. For WLCU I say thank you for giving me the opportunity to live the same positive experience all over again.

The writer with the Lebanese tour group May 2015 at the University of Notre Dame, Beirut, Lebanese Emigration Research Centre with the plaque commemorating the names of Lebanese who lost their lives on board the Titanic.

Lebanon: Forty-Six Interesting Facts

1. Lebanon has 18 religious communities.
2. Arabic is the official National language. French & English are also spoken.
3. It has 42 universities.
4. It has 40 daily newspapers.
5. It has over 100 banks (not branches of a bank).
6. 70% of students are in private schools.
7. 40% of the Lebanese people are Christians (this is the highest percentage of all the Arab countries), 54% are Muslims and 5.6% are Druze.
8. The name 'Lebanon' appears 69 times in the Old Testament.
9. Beirut was destroyed and rebuilt 7 times (this is why it is compared to the Phoenix which rises from the ashes).
10. There are approx. 6 Million Lebanese – including refugees – in Lebanon and around 12-16 million Lebanese and people of Lebanese descent outside Lebanon.
11. 'Sky Bar' was voted number 1 night club in the world.
12. Beirut is the 10th most popular shopping destination in the world.
13. Beirut was named "World Book Capital" in 2009.
14. Lebanon, the country, was occupied by over 14 countries (Egyptians – Hittites – Assyrians – Babylonians – Persians –Alexander the Great's Army – the Roman Byzantine Empire – the Arabian Peninsula – the Crusaders – Ottoman Empire – Britain – France – Israel – Syria).
15. Byblos is the oldest continuously inhabited city in the world.
16. Lebanon is the only Arab and Asian country that has absolutely no desert.
17. There are 15 rivers in Lebanon (all of them coming from its own mountains).
18. There are over 400 archaeological sites in Lebanon, making it one of countries in the world with the most archaeological sites.

19. The first alphabet was created in Byblos.
20. The only remaining temple of Jupiter (the main Roman god) is in Baalbek, Lebanon (The City of the Sun).
21. The name of the 'Bible' is derived from the Greek word for Byblos.
22. According to Christianity, Jesus performed his first miracle of turning water into wine in Cana, Lebanon.
23. The Phoenicians (original people of Lebanon) were the first great maritime people.
24. Phoenicians also reached America long before Christopher Columbus.
25. The first law school in the world was built in Downtown Beirut around AD 200.
26. People say that the cedar trees were planted by God's own hands. This is why they're called "The Cedars of God", and this is why Lebanon is called "God's Country on Earth".
27. The creators of Tom & Jerry are originally Lebanese (Joseph Barbara & William Hanna).
28. King Solomon's temple was built by King Hiram of Tyre with cedar trees from Lebanon.
29. Egypt's Pharaohs imported Lebanon's cedar trees, marble and timber.
30. Lebanon is the first Arab country that had a constitution.
31. Lebanon, which represents 2.5% of the total area of the Arabic Peninsula, produces 70% of the publications in the Arab world.
32. In springtime, and on the same day, you can ski in the mountains and/or swim in the sea.
33. "Ask not what your country can do for you, ask what you can do for your country". Most people associate this quote with a speech made by US President John F Kennedy in 1961. In fact, it came from one of Gibran Khalil Gibran's books. (Lebanese writer and artist).
34. The creator and the production manager of the iPod is originally Lebanese (Tony Fadel).
35. The Lebanese Hassan Kamel Al-Sabbah was a technological leader whose inventions in electricity had a great impact on the development of 20th century

technology and he was the first one who worked on creating electricity from sunlight.

36. "Work is Love made visible" is a quote by Kahlil Gibran.
37. There is recent evidence that the Phoenicians reached the Celtic world of Ireland and England.
38. Lebanon's National anthem 'Kulluna lil-Watan' means "All of us, for the country".
39. Lebanon is a small country, just 10,452 km^2.
40. In 2009 The New York Times rated Beirut the No.1 travel destination world-wide for its hospitality and nightlight.
41. Lebanon has a unique political system based on 'confessionalism'. The President is always a Maronite Christian, the Speaker of the House a Shiite Muslim and the Prime Minster a Sunni Muslim.
42. The largest expatriate Lebanese community lives in Brazil.
43. Maronites are the largest of the 12 Christian groups in Lebanon. Greek Orthodox are the second largest.
44. Lebanon is famous for its musical festivals which are held throughout the year.
45. Lebanon has six ski resorts.
46. 93% of the population are literate.

In the past flat roofs in Lebanon were covered with mud. When the mud started to crack the owners of the home would cover the roof with a fresh layer of mud and invite their neighbors to form a line and stamp their feet while walking on the roof to fix the mud.

Legend has it that this is how the *Dabke* – Lebanon's National dance – was created.

Lebanese Tertiary Education

An option for Lebanese South Africans

Perhaps one of the greatest problems facing parents in South Africa today is education, and in particular tertiary education. While South Africa has some outstanding universities, recent years have seen protests, unrest and disruption on campuses.

Tertiary education in Lebanon is, therefore, an option:

-There are 42 universities in Lebanon. A fact that may surprise readers and indeed the world.

-The top three or four Universities are of world standard: The University of Notre Dame, Beirut, the American University of Beirut and St Joseph's University.

-Gibran Kahlil Gibran was sent back to Lebanon from France to complete his tertiary education.

-There are Lebanese South Africans who have completed their tertiary education at, for example, The University of Notre Dame, and are very successful in South Africa today.

-Most Lebanese students are fluent in Arabic, French, and English. There are Universities that have English as their main language.

(Dedicated to my Mother Moiralinda Karam Kairouz, a great proponent of a Lebanese Education).

The Goat

"Lucky is he or she who has a goat's pen in the mountains of Lebanon".

Many of the older Lebanese South African families have at some stage had land issues in their native Lebanon, be it ground lost, bought or sold or simply abandoned. Some try hard to have ground registered in their name and others do not know where to start.

It has been stated that Lebanon, in its present state, would be very poorly off if it were not for the immigrant Lebanese. Estimated at 12-16 million, Lebanese in the Diaspora support their Motherland in various ways: sending money to their families, visiting Lebanon and spending hard earned money, and yet others have business dealings with their Motherland.

The Lebanese work hard to educate their children, who eventually emigrate.

What has this to do with a goat's pen? President of the World Lebanese Cultural Union (WLCU) Eid Chedrawi clearly stated when visiting South Africa: "All who have Lebanese citizenship must vote in the general elections". Every Lebanese in the Diaspora who can legally obtain a Lebanese passport must do so. It is not easy, but anything worthwhile is not easy.

Just like South Africa is the gateway to Africa, so Lebanon is the gateway to the oil rich Middle East. It is about business and business means money.
It is about securing the villages and a stake in the Holy Land. The universe is unlimited, but space on planet earth is limited. More so in Lebanon which is only 10,452 km^2.

What a wonderful experience for our youth to gain experience in another country, a tertiary education at a university in Lebanon. Lebanese South Africans are even having their weddings in Lebanon. Far better than on a beach in Cape Town or Mauritius.

A goat's pen in Lebanon is not as easy as it seems. It is a holistic approach, a challenge. Far harder than buying timeshare at Umhlanga Rocks, or putting up a high rise in Parkhurst in Johannesburg or even securing ground and property in Sandton.

Great progress has been made in creating our South African Lebanese "Goat pen": a school built in the South of Johannesburg (and God willing one in the North will follow); a Maronite mission in Umhlanga Rocks, and another in Krugersdorp with a regular monthly Mass and community get together. A community that prays and stays together creates a solid church.

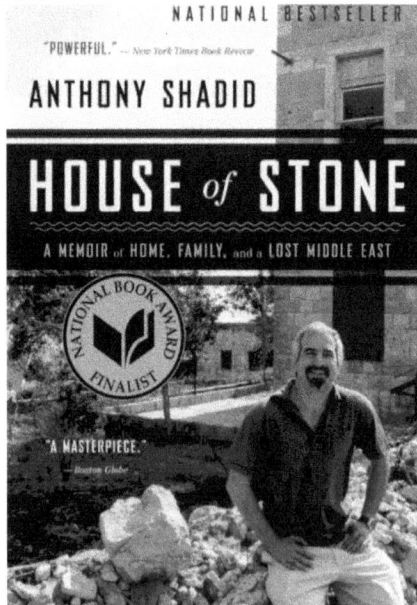

The late Anthony Shadid, twice Pulitzer Prize winner, penned this beautiful memoir, 'House of Stone' about his time in Lebanon renovating his ancestral home.

CHAPTER 7

Lebanese Spirituality

Saint Augustine

History prior to St Augustine

Christianity has its origin in Judaism. Judaism has its origin in Phoenicia (Lebanon). Islam has its origins in Judaism and Christianity.

The great virtues of pre Judaism (586 BC) are Phoenician.

The Feminine virtue was encapsulated in Dido of Carthage, a Phoenician princess, long before Judaism. It is of genuine Semitic origin, and not Pseudo Babylonian. It is embedded in a deep North African civilization which pagan Rome had to destroy.

Elissa, founder of Carthage

According to Roman and Greek sources Carthage was founded by Elissa (known as Dido – meaning wanderer – by the Romans) in what is today Tunisia, North Africa in circa 825 BC.

Elissa's father – the King of Tyre in Lebanon – had willed his Kingdom to both Elissa, a woman of extraordinary beauty, and her younger brother Pygmalion.

Elissa married the High Priest of Melkart who had secret treasures.

Pygmalion wanted the treasures so he killed Elissa's husband in order to seize his treasure.

Elissa – known as a model of wisdom, ambition and strong will – would not let him find it, so she fled taking the treasures with her.

She commissioned 80 Phoenician sailors and sailed to Cyprus, just off the Lebanese coast, where she recruited 80 Cypriot 'prostitutes' to accompany the Lebanese to Carthage, North Africa. Whilst history brands these woman as of ill repute, many were decent, ordinary attractive women who had fallen on bad times.

Legend goes that Elissa asked the Berber king Iarbas for a small piece of land – only as much as could be encompassed by an ox hide – for a temporary refuge. Cleverly – as the story goes – Elissa then cut the hide into small strips laid it out and demarcated a large area which was the foundation of the great Carthaginian Empire of history.

Just as 70 Israelites entered Egypt and formed a nation four hundred years earlier, Elissa, with herself as leader, and 80 Lebanese men and 80 Cypriot women, formed the nucleus of the greatest Empire of the then modern world.

Saint Augustine and his writings

Augustine of Hippo – 13 November 354 to 28 August 430 – was an early North African Christian theologian and philosopher whose writings influenced the development of Western Christianity and philosophy.

He was the Bishop of Hippo Regis in North Africa and is viewed as one of the most important Church Fathers in Western Christianity for his writings in the Patristic era – early Christianity.

Amongst his most important works are "The City of God" and "Confessions".

Augustine lived in a time of social turmoil: an empire in freefall, the rise of barbarism, a crisis of reason. In our times (2017) we see similar crises: civil wars in Syria and South Sudan; the hint of the break-up of one global bloc (the European Union); the weakening of a superpower, the United States of America, through internal political turmoil; nuclear brinkmanship in East Asia; and populist irrationality and fundamentalism on every continent.

In response to his times Augustine wrote "The City of God". By stressing the difference between the Heavenly City and the Human City, Augustine offers believers a hope rooted in realism.

His genius lay in reminding Christians that we have a duty to live in the human city, with our eyes on the Heavenly City. An eye on the main prize.

"Confessions", Augustine's autobiographical works of 13 books written in Latin between AD 397 and 400, outlines his sinful youth and conversion to Christianity. It is seen as the first autobiography ever written and one of the great masterpieces of Western Literature.

In AD 313, just 43 years before Augustine, Christianity was legalized by Emperor Constantine of Rome.

For three centuries before this, Christianity was a religion of active non-violence.

Constantine threw out the "Sermon on the Mount" and the commandment to love one's enemies and turned to the pagan Cicero to justify Christian violence – the so called 'just war'.

In April 2016 the Church turned towards non-violence with an unprecedented meeting at the Vatican.

Council of Carthage

On the 28th of August 397 Augustine was 43 years of age.

He was the prime mover at the Council of Carthage, a milestone in deciding what would be included in the Bible, and had this to say about the Gospel:

> *"I shall not believe in the Gospel itself if the authority of the Catholic Church did not move me to do so."*

"If you believe what you like in the Gospel, and reject what you do not like, it is not the Gospel you believe in, but yourself".

He ends his "Confessions" with the following beautiful reminder:

> *"Thou hast made us for Thyself, oh Lord, and our heart is restless until it finds its rest in Thee".*

Augustine University

There is a University in the City of Johannesburg named after Saint Augustine, whose Rector and President is Father Michael Van Heerden, who has done the mission during Holy Week at the Church of Our Lady of Lebanon in the South of Johannesburg.

Catholics have great confidence in their faith and never criticize or belittle any religion.

The University of Saint Augustine, proved this by having a lecture on "Atheism" given by a prominent agnostic from the University of the Witwatersrand in 2012, who argued that atheism makes for a happier individual than theism.

Great stuff. But as Father Yves Lejour, a great friend of the Lebanese community in South Africa, says: "Sincere, but perhaps sincerely wrong."

But what does Saint Augustine say? The spiritual "Home of the Soul", says St. Augustine, is built up in time and dedicated in eternity.

> *"Faith is the Foundation. Hope the walls, Charity the roof or covering. The sacraments are the great means of grace. The chief instruments required for the building. The virtues, the Christian rule of Life. The daily exercises may be likened to the adornment and furniture, and paintings in the home"[7].*

May your spiritual home be comfortable, tasteful and happy.

Saint Augustine's Punic Ancestry

Was St Augustine Lebanese? According to the great Scholars of the Church, Saint Augustine was of Phoenician, Latin and Berber descent.

His mother - Saint Monica was born in 322 in Tagaste (in modern day Turkey) of Christian parents. In the West St Monica is considered the patron Saint of wives and mothers whose sons have gone astray – as she prayed constantly for both her husband and the wayward Augustine in his early years – both of whom converted to Christianity.

---

[7] A Summary of Christian Doctrine: A Popular Presentation of the Teachings of the Bible; New King James Edition by Edward W.A. Koehler, Revised Edition; 1971

But it is not what others say about Saint Augustine's Ancestry that counts, it is what Saint Augustine himself said. Saint Augustine considers himself to be Punic.

Punic refers both to early Carthage (Kingdom in North Africa, founded by the Phoenicians) and to the Semitic language spoken there, which was a dialect of Phoenician and survived until circa 500, 70 years after St Augustine's death.

Punic comes from the Classical Punicus – early Carthage. This is properly Phoenician from 'Phoeni' the Classical Greek 'Phoenix' which means Phoenician. Phoenician = Lebanese.

So we can surmise that Saint Augustine spoke with a Phoenician accent, and that our beloved Father Michael Chebli, who gave me the outline of this book, was correct.

Saint Augustine was a Punic African. Just as Moses was an Israelite African slave. A son of Africa. Just like all South Africans of Lebanese descent, our children and grandchildren.

If Saint Augustine was alive today, he could apply for Lebanese citizenship.

We, the Lebanese, now take leave of our Saint Augustine, of our brothers and sisters in the West.

We leave them with Rome. The three treaties of Martin Luther. The selected writings of Marx and Engels. The Russian Revolution of 1917. 10 days that shook the world. History of the Jewish people in Europe, Solomon Grayzel. The Spanish Inquisition. Henry the Eighth. The Westphalia Treaty (which ended the European War on Religion: 1618 to 1648).

We turn now to Saint Maron, Lebanon, and the Lebanese influence in the East.

St. Maron Patron Saint of the Lebanese (Maronite) Christian Church

St Maron was born in a small town called Cyrrhus near Antioch around 350 AD.

Like many spiritual seekers and holy people, Maron was drawn to the high mountains, choosing as his home a ruined Pagan temple high on the Semaan Mountain between Antioch (present day Turkey) and Aleppo (present day Iraq).

Here, on the deserted mountain, he followed the life of a simple hermit. After cleansing it from devils, St Maron used the temple for Holy Mass and offerings of the Holy Eucharist, while spending his time in the open, praying and fasting. He became famous in the area for his faith, holiness and healing powers. His countless miracles attracted thousands of believers who sought his advice and help.

St. Maron was an excellent preacher and ardent believer in Christ and in Christianity. He was a passionate missionary who sought not only to cure physical ailments, but also had a great charism for nurturing and healing "lost souls", both pagan and Christian. St. John of Chrysostom sent him a letter around 405 AD expressing his great love and respect and asking St. Maron to pray for him.

St. Maron's way was deeply monastic and mystic with emphasis on the spiritual and ascetic aspects of living. For him, all was connected to God and God was connected to all. St. Maron embraced the quiet solitude of mountain life.

He lived in the open air exposed to the forces of nature, and his extraordinary desire to know God's presence in all things allowed him to transcend these forces and discover an intimate union with God. He was able to free himself from the physical world by his passion and eagerness for prayer and enter into a mystical relationship of love with the creator.

St. Maron attracted hundreds of monks and priests who came to live with him and become his disciples and followers. They preached the Bible in the Antioch Empire (present day Syria, Lebanon, Turkey, Iraq, Jordan and Israel), and built hundreds of churches, abbeys and schools. They were known far and wide for their faith, devotion and perseverance.

At the age of seventy, in the year AD 410, and after completing his holy mission, St. Maron died peacefully surrounded by his disciples and followers.

Maronity through the ages

The Maronite Rite takes its name from this holy hermit, however Christianity took root in Lebanon before the Maronites.

Saint Paul – on his 3rd apostolic journey – landed at Tyre, where he founded a substantial Christian Community.

> *"We looked up the disciples and stayed there for seven days. Through the Spirit they told Paul not to go on to Jerusalem. When our days there were ended, we left and proceeded on our journey; and all of them, with wives and children, escorted us outside the city. There we knelt down on the beach and prayed. (Acts 21:4-5)*

The Maronite Movement reached Lebanon when Saint Maron's first disciple, Abraham of Cyrrhus,, born c350 in present day Turkey (called the Apostle of Lebanon), realised that paganism was still thriving in Lebanon, and so he set out to convert the pagans to Christianity by introducing them to the way of Saint Maron.

By the 4th Century a basilica was built on the site of the former Temple of Melkart. The Maronites remained faithful to the teachings of the Catholic Church.

The Christian communities flourished in Tyre and other Lebanese cities for four centuries, and were especially vigorous in the mountainous area of Lebanon during the 4th, 5th and 6th centuries AD.

Lebanon Northern Maronite Society

In the late 8th Century AD a group of Christians known as Mardaites (also Jarajima) settled in North Lebanon. This followed the order of the Byzantine Emperor.

Their mission was to raid Islamic territories in Syria.

The first Philosopher to mention the Mardaites was Theophanes who relates that in 669 they attacked Lebanon and occupied portions of the country stretching from the Black mountains to the "Holy City" of Jerusalem.

They also occupied the mountains of North Lebanon where they were joined by slaves, both captive and free. They merged with the local population, refusing to leave after the Emperor struck a deal with the Muslim Caliph of Damascus.

They thus became part of Maronite Society.

In 1291, after the fall of Acre (in present day Occupied Palestine/Israel), the last Crusader outpost in the Levant, the remnants of the European settlers who succeeded in escaping capture by the Mamluks also settled in North Lebanon and became part of the Maronite Society.

Monasticism and the Monasteries

To understand early Maronity we have to understand monasticism and the monastery.

After St Maron's death a great monastery called Beit Maron was built in AD 452 on the Orontes River which flourished for 500 years

So the Maronites have been Catholic long before the great schism of orthodoxy in AD 1054. There is a strong tradition amongst Maronites that they never lacked, or lost, communion with the Holy See.

Maronite monks and their followers in the remote mountains of Lebanon began to develop a distinct identity as a church. The Maronite Church became a formal entity with the institution of the Maronite Patriarchate of Antioch in the 7th Century. They elected a bishop as their head who took the title of Patriarch of Antioch and all the East.

The first Patriarch was Saint John Maron chosen in AD 685. He was affirmed by Pope Sergius I, highlighting that the Maronite Church was in communion with Rome from the beginning.

From approximately 700 to 1367 the Maronites experienced a period of an independent homeland with Maronite Churches and Monasteries flourishing in relative safety and isolation.

This explains why Maronites have such respect for their clergy and why the Maronite Church will always be the hub of our lives and why the President of Lebanon will (please God) continue to be a Maronite Christian.

It was only in the 12th Century that Maronites came into contact with the Latin Church.

Between 1367 and 1516 the Mamluk Kingdom (ex-slaves) ruled the Maronite Christians.

In the 16th Century we saw the conquest of the Maronite homeland by the Turks and the beginning of the long centuries of Ottoman domination from 1516 to 1918.

A major reform took place in 1736 when the Church drafted an almost complete Canon (rules) for the Maronite Church, created a regular diocesan structure for the first time, and established the Maronite ecclesiastical life that endures to this day.

The Maronite Patriarchs have resided at Bkerke about 39 Km from Beirut since 1790. Today (2017) there are ten dioceses in Lebanon with over 800 parishes and seven other jurisdictions in the Middle East.

Maronite Prayer

By the intercession of your Mother, O Lord, turn your wrath from the land and its inhabitants. Put an end to trouble and sedition, banish from it war, plunder, hunger and plague. Have pity on us in our misfortunes. Console those of us who are sick. Help us in our weakness. Deliver us from oppression and exile. Grant eternal rest to our dead. Allow us to live in peace in this world that we may glorify you.

The Maronites of the Expansion

Due to Ottoman rule, famine, disease and war we witnessed great waves of migration of Lebanese – and Maronites in particular – to the four corners of the globe especially to the Americas, Africa and Australia. In every country in which they have settled they have created flourishing communities.

Many of the approximately 12 - 16 million Lebanese in The Diaspora today, are of Maronite descent.

The Lebanese needed 150 years to learn, assimilate, influence and dedicate themselves to prepare for their great vision and mission in the 21st Century: The Inheritance.

Spirit of Maronity

As we have seen the Maronites made Lebanon their home from the 4th Century. They were and still are a united entity; hopeful, faithful and strong believers in the Christian Catholic doctrine. They make victories of defeat, joy of sorrow and hope of despair.

They successfully created, with hard work, faith and sacrifice, the Maronite nation, by fulfilling its four basic pillars: a land, a people, a civilization and a politically independent entity.

The Maronites established the state of Lebanon and made it an oasis for the persecuted in the area. They believed and practiced – and still do – multiculturalism and pluralism. They created with the help of other minorities in the Middle East the unique nation of Lebanon.[8]

---

[8] *The section on Maronity draws – with gratitude – on the writing of Elias Bejjani, Chairman for the Canadian Lebanese Coordinating Council (LCCC) Human Rights activist, journalist & political commentator. Spokesman for the Canadian Lebanese Human Rights Federation (CLHRF)*

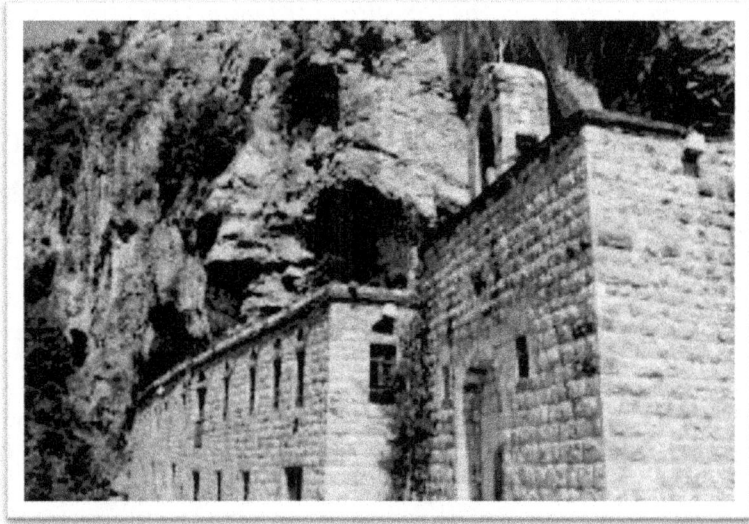

Monastery in the Holy Qadisha Valley

Maronity

*According to Lebanese Maronite historian, Fouad
Afram al-Boustani, 1906-1995, Maronity is a faith
of intelligence, an identification of life , a solid
belief in Catholicism, a love for others, an ongoing
struggle for righteousness, a mentality of
openness to the whole world, and its different
civilizations, and a vehicle for martyrdom.*

Vatican Council II

Our Maronite ancestors overcame great persecution to protect their Church and faith. Out of their experience developed a superb liturgy and many beautiful traditions. We are called by the Universal Catholic Church to protect those traditions.

In a beautiful apostolic letter Blessed Pope John Paul II declared:

> *"...I listen to the Churches of the East, which I know are living interpreters of the treasure of tradition they preserve. In contemplating it, before my eyes appear elements of great significance for fuller and more thorough understanding of the Christian experience...the Christian East has a unique and privileged role as the original setting where the Church was born"*

The Vatican Council is very clear on the Eastern Rite Catholics, including the Maronites.

We have a very special vocation in that we are from the Holy Land, and have a duty and responsibility to maintain and uphold our Spiritual Heritage, our Ecclesiastical discipline and our Rite.

Not only for ourselves, but for the whole world.

Vatican Council II clearly demonstrates that the universal Church must assist us in this calling and vocation.

Catholic Ecumenical Councils include 21 Councils over a period of 1700 years.

They are assemblies of Patriarchs, Cardinals, residing Bishops, Abbots, and male heads of religious orders and other juridical persons nominated by the Pope.

The purpose of an ecumenical council is to define doctrine, reaffirm truths and rout out heresy. In order to be valid, council decisions must be approved by the Pope.

To make the Apostolic work more effective, Vatican Council II was held between 11th October 1962 and 8th December 1965. The theme was "The Catholic Church and the Modern World".

The author (left) with the Lebanese Patriarch. H.E. Boutros Bechara el Rahi, at the Lebanese Embassy in Johannesburg 2016

Here we focus on the decree on the Eastern Catholic Churches, as it affects the Maronites of Lebanon.

"Those who by reason of their office or apostolic ministry have frequent dealings with the Eastern Churches, or their faithful should be instructed as their office demands in theoretical and practical knowledge of the rites, discipline, doctrine, history, and character of the members of the Churches".

He adds, that they should set up so far as is possible, houses or even provinces of the Eastern Rite, to make their Apostolic work more effective"[9].

---

[9] Preservation of the Spiritual Heritage of the Eastern Churches. Page 443, Section 5. Vatican Council II. The Conciliar and Post Conciliar Documents, by Austin Flannery O.P. General Editor. Prefaced by John Cardinal Wright.

The statue of Maronite Saint Maron, outside the Vatican in Rome evidences the close relationship between Maronite Christians and the Catholic Church

People of the Cedars and Minimalism

"Be content with your little, whilst the fool seeks more" so quotes the late Jessie Paola, "Cedar Leaf" correspondent.

We live by the clock today. We spend eight hours earning money, eight hours spending 150% of what has been earned, and most of the remaining eight hours wondering why we can't sleep. So says Hugh Allen, a community financier and micro finance lender. His company is VSLA (Village Savings and Loan Association).

According to Worldwide Magazine, a Catholic Publication appearing bimonthly by the Comboni Missionaries of The Heart of Jesus, South Africa, when people become self-centred and self-enclosed, our greed increases. The emptier a person's heart, the more he or she needs to buy, own and consume.

This Consumerism is considered by Pope Francis to be one of the great scourges facing humanity. The others being the arms race and the destruction of the planet. The arms race does two things: makes a lot of money for the dealers, and kills innocent men, women and children.

The antitheses of Consumerism are Minimalism and Spirituality. Let us look at how the Lebanese (almost unwittingly) embraced minimalism.

Firstly, let us look at Lebanon. As we have seen, it is a very small country, only about half the size of the Kruger National Park in South Africa. But the Lebanese care for their small little patch and every piece of arable land is developed.

It may be small, but it has a big heart. The Lebanese – including those who are not affluent, indeed even the poor – are renowned for being among the most hospitable people on the planet.

Lebanon has been a haven of the oppressed throughout the ages and is currently home to in the region of 2 million Palestinian and Syrian refugees.

In fact, it is estimated that today one in four Lebanese is a refugee. During December 2012 the United Nation praised Lebanese families for taking in more than a third of the 160,000 Syrian refugees who streamed into Lebanon escaping the civil war in neighbouring Syria.

Once again, when we look at the Lebanese in South Africa, we see how we were initially forced into a subsistence lifestyle. Most immigrants from Lebanon were poor, often peasant farmers, unable to speak the local languages and with meagre possessions. A minority within a minority.

With the pressures of victimization, materialism was not on the agenda. It was survival at all costs.

But when life started going well, there was the lure of the love of horses and the gamble. Because, sadly, human nature is totally against minimalism. People want more and more. One poor lady, born in Mayfair, who prospered later, boasted of owning 700 pairs of shoes!

But because of the influence of the great leadership of Father Peter Alam and Father Michael Chebli – Maronite Lebanese Missionaries whose faith is based on mysticism, prayer and the monastic life – the "People of the Cedars" in South Africa had a strong spiritual and moral anchor.

The older generations instilled into our psyches the mentality of the people of the mountains: No waste in their kitchens and in their homes. Always making do with little.

In 2015, when I led a group of 15 South Africans on a heritage pilgrimage to our ancestral homeland, we experienced spirituality and minimalism first hand.

We began our journey in the Holy Qadisha valley region where the saints and the people lived in safety and security in their mountain strongholds.

Here we visited the monasteries, caves and homes of the mountaineers and saw their simple, minimalist lifestyle – focused on community, service and spirituality – not possessions.

We also had the privilege of witnessing cooperation between Christian and Muslim communities in the South of Lebanon. Both inheritors of the "People of the Cedars".

We visited Notre Dame University in Beirut, where intellectual Lebanese are synthesizing a philosophy, vision and mission for the Lebanese worldwide. A people geared to dialogue between civilizations, cultures and religions.

And we can add a 'sacred world economy' which focusses on a gradual, planned reduction of the arms race (because if immediate, world economies would collapse) and preservation of our sacred planet for our descendants.

In radical contrast we also saw the glitzy commercial "High Life" in Jounieh and Beirut, where those who choose can 'shop till they drop'.

So, as "People of the Cedars" we have two choices: consumerism, greed and materialism, or minimalism and the spirituality as taught by our ancestors in the Holy Cedars.

You decide.

To Sing God's Praises is to Pray Twice: James Nunan

22 August 1935- 23 June 2013

Like most who live in the Northern suburbs of Johannesburg, I dutifully attended 'Phantom of the Opera' at the Teatro at Montecasino together with my granddaughter who was 10 at the time. When I asked what she thought of the Opera, she replied that it frightened both her and her 13 year old friend.

Quite frankly, apart from a few numbers, I did not enjoy the show; in fact at interval I thought the show was over. Not so and again, dutifully, I watched the second half.

One must always compare apples with apples – the lead man in the show and one of the lead singers at the Maronite Church. On Good Friday, during communion, James Nunan did a rendition of the hymn, "Sweet Sacrament Divine", one of the most beautiful hymns I have ever heard. James had a soprano voice and was one of the great singers in the Catholic Diocese of Johannesburg.

James had been singing since the age of seven, and had no doubt that his gift was an anointing – a gift from God.

After Holy Mass, we continued our Good Friday service with Stations of the Cross. We climbed 'the mountain' (which is actually a hill) adjacent to the Church of Our Lady of Lebanon in Mulbarton, just South of Johannesburg, where we enjoyed a picnic at the top.

An exercise of both body and soul.

In February 2018, Pope Francis met with Maronite seminarians and priests from Lebanon studying in Rome. He said their mission is preparing to sow peace in the Middle East, and that Lebanon serves as an example of peaceful coexistence between Christians and Muslims.

POPE FRANCIS

"You all, in a special way, are called to serve everyone as brothers, above all feeling like everyone's brothers. Supporting each other using what you've learned, act so that Lebanon always practices its vocation as a light for the region's people and a sign of peace that comes from God."

In addition, Pope Francis asked them to cultivate a life of prayer and ambitious internal struggle, to put themselves truly at the service of those who need their help. As a memento, they presented the Holy Father with a sculpture of Saint Maron made of Lebanese cedar that contains one of the saint's relics (photograph below)

Priest and the Poet by Ken Hanna

Dedicated to: Father Michael Chebli, who served the Lebanese Community in SA from 1962-2005, and Gibran Kahlil Gibran – poet, writer, artist and mystic of the Mountains of Lebanon, 1883 to 1931.

When is the priest a poet, and the poet a priest?
I have seen the priest in the poet and the poet in the priest.
It is a touching of the heart.
It is the constant awareness of a holy presence.
A turning towards Truth, Beauty and the Eternal.
It is a state of near purity.
Let us feel with the priest; and love the poet,
And love the "One" who inspires them.
It is the joy of the spirit dancing within them –
A state of almost perpetual euphoria.
And yet it is only for a short while.
The priest and the poet as if by some hidden power are turned off.
Grow silent. Not to be seen or felt.
A desert experience, a period of aridness and desolation.
Priest and Poet experiencing the same phenomenon.
They pray, they think, they ponder, they love and they heal.
They heal you with your gift of tears and you heal them with your gift of love.
And you look for the wholeness of your fellow human being.
Fulfilment in your surroundings and your workplace.
Ah, the poet again: Philosopher, Thinker, Lover of mankind.
His heart cries out to the Spirit: Please heal, make whole.
And the priest again, realizing the imperfection within himself,
Struggles to capture the "Ecstasy of the Holy One".
When will it come again?
He kneels in the solitude of prayer.
And fasts and does penance.
He walks out into the light and suddenly it hits him:
There it is. The same Spirit in the beggar on the streets.
The poet reflects, the priest touches.
The poet grieves and cries for the poor.
The priest draws him out of his misery, shows him another way.
The poet feels, and walks away.
The priest struggles and stays to face another day.

CHAPTER 7

Lebanese Customs and Traditions

All strong, cohesive communities have their unique, idiosyncratic traditions and customs that strengthen ties of love and understanding–some meaningful and sacred; others secular and (sometimes) quirky, which are passed down from generation to generation. Here are some of ours (with grateful thanks to my sister Moira Farah).

Those related to Maronite Christianity

"Arbeen – Fourty Days" – Honouring of the Dead

- After a loved one has died, *'Bagoor'* an Aramaic prayer/chant for the Dead is led by the priest at the home of the deceased before the funeral. After a 40-day mourning period, a special Holy Mass is offered for the deceased. This reflects the period that Jesus Christ suffered in the desert. Holy Mass is again offered in honour of the deceased a year after his/her death.
- Weeks before Christmas, Lebanese plant chick peas or lentils on a piece of cotton wool and water daily. Once grown they are used for the manger of the Nativity scene.
- Christmas trees are decorated with orange peels cut into different shapes.
- The cake *maamoul* means "filled" and is traditionally eaten on the days before Lent, Easter Sunday and the feast of Epiphany. The wooden mold used to make *maamoul* symbolizes Jesus' Cross; the pattern around the Cross symbolizes the sponge with which Jesus was given vinegar to drink and the sweet filling – the Resurrection – hence the meaning 'filled'.

- During Epiphany (also known as 'Three Kings Day' in reference to the Three Wise Men) Lebanese keep the outside light of our homes on and greet each other by saying 'Deyim Deyim" (to wish others blessings all year long). We prepare dough with yeast filled with coins which we hang outside our homes in a small bag. We believe that Christ will pass by at midnight (hence the light being kept on) and will bless our dough balls with abundance.
- Whenever the Lebanese make Kibbe or dough for bread/pies, we always make a Cross on the mixture – a blessing symbolic of the fish and bread Our Lord fed to the multitudes.
- Lebanese do not fast on the day of The Resurrection, it is our day of celebration.
- To have a clean heart for the fast during Lent (and to avoid ants in the home), Lebanese thoroughly clean our homes on Ash Monday (also referred to as Clean Monday).
- 'Harissi' – a special lamb's neck stew is made to celebrate the patron Saint of each village on their feast day in the villages of Lebanon.
- A sour soup – 'rishti' is made on Good Friday.

Lebanon's National Dance: The Dabke

The 'Evil Eye' or Blue Bean is frowned upon by the Church as it is a Lebanese superstition (not a tradition). It is regarded as the manifestation of envy/jealousy and believed to protect children. That is why Lebanese always say, "Ismisalieb" or "Smala" after a compliment.

Palm Sunday – *Shaanineh*

On Palm Sunday we take our children and grandchildren to celebrate Holy Mass and the special procession, while they happily carry candles decorated with lilies and roses.

Men, women and children hold palm fronds with olive branches and actively participate in the palm procession with modesty, love and joy; rejoicing loudly:

"Hosanna to the son of David. Blessed is he who comes in the name of the Lord. Hosanna in the highest."
Matthew 21:9.

Children

-To determine the sex of the child, the husband places his wedding ring on a strand of his wife's hair and lets it swing to and fro over her belly. To the right a girl, to the left a boy.
-When a child is born, Lebanese prepare *Meghli* (a traditional rice pudding decorated with almonds).
-When the cord of a newborn baby falls off Lebanese bury the cord in the garden, light incense and pray for the child's protection.
-First born boys are always named after their grandfather.
-Lebanese woman rest for the first forty days after giving birth as we say in this time their graves are open.

.....and a few more

-Lebanese people believe that those who don't drink 'ahweh', strong Lebanese coffee, will lose their nationality.
-Time in Lebanon is not usually considered a valued commodity. Being late is common practice – even a sign of being fashionable.
-Raising the eyebrows and nodding the head are used to say 'No'.
-It is Lebanese tradition to take flowers, sweet pastries and alcohol when visiting people. Gifts must always be handed with the right hand.
-Lebanese woman sing *Zalaouta* (loud pitched cries) as a way of expressing happiness.
-Lebanese believe if a bird flies into our home good news is on the way.
-If Lebanese break a glass we say "Nkassar el charr", meaning breaking a bad spell, and if we spill coffee it's a sign of "Kheyr" – a blessing.
-Three kisses on the cheeks are given in greeting.

Weddings

-There is a 'bathing of the bride' tradition in South African Lebanese culture. In Lebanon they have a pre-wedding celebration hosted by their families.
-There is no Kitchen/Linen Tea or the giving of gifts party in Lebanon. It is customary for the Groom to open a bank account for guests to give gifts of cash. Bank details are always included in the invitation and the lowest amount given is $100.
-At a Lebanese wedding the groom's parents present their future daughter-in-law with a gold or diamond piece of jewelry to wear on her wedding day.
-The Lebanese wedding cake is always cut with a sword and it is traditional to have Zaffe (Lebanese dancers surrounded by drums).

Conclusion

Lebanon and the world of the Lebanese Diaspora find ourselves in a unique position and situation today.

Lebanon, the Motherland, is the centre and the playground of world political, economic and religious dynamics in the Holy Land.

Lebanon and the Lebanese have suffered devastating persecution, civil war and occupations over the centuries. Despite, or perhaps because of, this we are a Nation endeavouring with courage and fortitude to become an example of religious and political respect and tolerance.

Despite failures, we continue striving to live, love and pray in harmony. We aspire to multi-culturalism and pluralism, to community-development and peace-building, religious acceptance and interfaith dialogue and understanding as exemplified in the Lebanese Dialogue Initiative (LDI).

In the Diaspora – so near yet so far – just a day away from Lebanon with modern travel, we have created vibrant, flourishing and strong communities. Through innovative programmes, such as "The Lebanese Diaspora Energy" (LDE) Initiative, we create and nurture friendships and networks of economic, professional and political support across the globe, remaining committed to both Lebanon and our adopted homelands.

We are dazed with the magnitude of the political, economic and social pressures on Lebanon. But despite trials and sorrows, our optimism and spirit in the Motherland and the Diaspora remain inexhaustible.

Lebanon is the Phoenix of the Middle East, rising again and again from the ashes of war. And like our Phoenician ancestors we sail ever onward, in search of new lands of hope and possibility.

Lebanity is our compass; faith the wind in our sails. The sailors each Lebanese woman and man committed to the vision of a strong, united and flourishing nation. Our sights always set on the shores of peace and inclusivity.

We are Lebanon: "The "People of the Cedars".

Striving to embody – as best we can – our values of Family, Faith, Finance and Fellowship; Dialogue; Unity in diversity; Heritage and Hospitality.

This is the dynamic world of the Lebanese.

Our unique and Sacred Vocation:

The Inheritance.

ABOUT THE AUTHOR:
Ken Hanna

Ken (left) receiving an award from Dr Guita Hourani (centre) and Director of the International Affairs Office at Notre Dame University, Beirut, Dr. Pierre Gedeon, in 2014

Ken Hanna is a Lebanese South African, and has Lebanese Citizenship.

He is Author of the Book "People of the Cedars: a 20th Century Insight into the Lebanese South African Community", edited by Father Charbel Habchi of the Lebanese Maronite Missionaries, 2011.

He is the recipient of three World Awards:

In 2007 he was honoured by the World Lebanese Cultural Union (WLCU) with the Golden Emigrant Award, in Brazil.

In 2014 he received an award from the Lebanese Emigration Research Centre (LERC) at the University of Notre Dame, Beirut for documenting Lebanese history in South Africa.

In 2016 he was named Lebanese Man of the Year by the Lebanese Heritage Foundation, Vancouver, WLCU.

Ken has visited Lebanon, Syria, Occupied Palestine (Israel) and Egypt. He honours his ancestors of history.